Sandy shows us how   ...
experiences are packed with punch as she teaches how to
navigate your own life challenges with humor and practical
application activities. *Passport to Freedom* is a true gift.

-Karen Eagle PhD., Professor of Entrepreneurship

As a medical professional with decades of clinical work I was
intrigued by Sandy's perspective of "thriving with cancer".
She effectively shares her life experiences and lessons learned
that enhance her resilience throughout her cancer journey.
This is a practical and often humorous guide to assist anyone on his or her own challenging journey. I suggest all my
patients and the doctors that treat them read this book.

-Sandy True, RN/FNP, PhD.

It has been said that strength does not come from winning.
When you go through hardships and decide not to surrender, that is strength. Sandy is the epitome of this belief
and more. Her ability to not just survive, but thrive during struggle is not only inspirational - but as she explains
in this book... attainable. From finding your WHY, to
embracing the suck, to harnessing flow states, this is a
must read for anyone looking for both inspiration and
tools. There is tremendous wisdom in these pages--enjoy
it and use it.

-Rich Diviney, Navy SEAL Officer (Ret.)
and Start With WHY Igniter

Passport to Freedom is simultaneously inspired and inspiring. Sandy herself embodies the elements of courage, grit and resilience, along with a dose of quirky (in a good way), being fully human, and a terrific sense of adventure. And, oh, by the way, Sandy is an incredible model for learning to use your intuition. She's a terrific teacher for helping you discover an extraordinary way to dance with life's journey, and not just cancer!

-Suzan K. Thompson, Ph.D., Licensed Professional Counselor (Virginia)

Through her 'sassy' and inspiring story, Sandy Travis reveals how to not only thrive through cancer, but through all of life. Hers is a stirring testimonial on what it means to live full out – turning upheaval into adventure; directing the power of the mind and heart; and keeping a sense of humor through it all. Her practical tips and exercises are so engaging and practical, I will read this book again – and I don't have cancer."

-Rev. Paula Mekdeci, Senior Minister, Unity Renaissance of Chesapeake, VA

What amazed us at our company was how Sandy turned her cancer news into something transformative. Her response lifted us up. It bonded us as a unit. And there is no doubt in my mind that Sandy's strength has been a significant factor in our addressing difficult business challenges— and turning them into amazing success. Sandy's signature inspiration is all over accomplishments. And it is imbued in the pages of this book.

-Christopher Naughton, Host & Executive Producer of *The American Law Journal*

Passport to Freedom is rich, deep and inspirational! While acknowledging and embracing both the ups and downs of the journey, Sandy kept moving forward and did not allow the fear of the major cancer diagnosis to consume her. She shares her amazing demonstration of using the HeartMath tools in real time to shift her emotions to facilitate healing on all levels and build her own inner resilience capacity. She is tenacious compassion in action both for herself and others facing their own "two-by-eights". Enjoy the book and facilitate your own insights and wisdom.

-Tricia Hoffman, Director, Training & Licensing, HeartMath LLC

Sandy has been an integral member of The Honor Foundation family ever since we kicked off our Special Operations Forces community Career Transition Institute in Virginia Beach, VA. She is an inspiring model of resilience. Her dedication to our mission and vision has been unsurpassed even in the midst of dealing with a significant cancer diagnosis. This book chronicles her journey, adaptability and insights and is a must read for anyone facing their own call to take their life to the next level and meet their challenges head-on.

-Jeff Pottinger, Chief Operating Officer, The Honor Foundation

I highly recommend this book to anyone with cancer who is learning how to thrive, and to those in their lives who need to be resilient in supporting and understanding their journey. Passport is an excellent resource for physicians, mental health counselors; coaches and mentors who want an inside look at maneuvering the ups and downs of a sudden traumatic life event.

-Michele Lash M.Ed., ATR, BCB Senior Fellow, Registered Psychotherapist

I could not put this book down. It captures the heart and mind. Sandy's indomitable spirit has been a real inspiration to me as I have watched her cancer journey. In addition to being a badass adventure story *Passport* gives you perspective and tools you can use in approaching your own life challenges and two-by-eights, whatever they may be.

-Michele Ewing, US Naval Officer (Ret.)

Passport is full of invaluable gems, tips and suggestions for moving from surviving to thriving when an unexpected two-by-eight hits. As a psychologist who has worked with various clinical and consulting clients, I have been deeply impressed with Sandy's resilience. She demonstrates not only a great capacity to shift limiting attitudes and actions that can block healing, but also shows us how to find deep meaning and purpose along the way! Highly, highly recommend her book!

-Ann Hammond, PhD.

PASSPORT TO FREEDOM

PASSPORT TO FREEDOM

Courage and Resilience on your Cancer Journey

Sandy Travis

ISBN-13: 9780692947951
ISBN-10: 0692947957
Library of Congress Control Number: 2017954190
StellarConnectionsIX, Virginia Beach, VA

HeartMath^R is a registered trademark of Quantum Intech Inc. For all
HeartMath^R trademarks, go to www.heartmath.com/trademarks.

To my amazing sister, Tina, and her family, Gene, Travis, and Brandon, who have always loved and accepted me on my quirky adventures, including this cancer journey. I could not have done it without you!

You can't stop the waves, but you can learn to surf.

—Jon Kabat-Zinn

No lifeguard on duty.

Contents

Introduction· xvii

**Part One: Notes from the Field on a
Yearlong Adventure** ·1
The Context: Posttraumatic Growth · · · · · · · · · · · · ·3
The Trigger ·6
Fumbling Forward Using My Intuition · · · · · · · · · · ·11
Conversations with Buddha · · · · · · · · · · · · · · · · · · 16
Words Matter—Choose Them Wisely· · · · · · · · · · · 19
Symbols Matter Too! ·23
"You Are One of Us, and We Take Care of
Our Own" · 25
"Embrace the Suck" · 30
Wigged Out, or How I Became a
Redhead Overnight · 33
I Have Other Alligators Closer to the Boat· · · · · · · · 37
Synchronicity: Show Me You've Got My Back · · · · · · 39
Giving, Receiving, and I Will Be Happy When... · · · 43

Divine Appointments · 46

"Yes, and…": Lessons from
Improvisational Theater · 48

Compassion, Compassion, Compassion · · · · · · · · · · · 51

Engage Your Heart · 54

Your Why Matters! · 60

What the *!@!*—You Want Me to Be Grateful? · · · · · 64

Two Wolves · 67

Happy Dance or Miracle? · 68

Taking Total Responsibility · · · · · · · · · · · · · · · · · · · 70

A Labyrinth or a Maze? · 74

Service as Healing · 77

I Am Human Too! · 79

Curing, Healing, and Survivor's Guilt · · · · · · · · · · · 81

Are You Waiting for the Other Shoe to Drop? · · · · · · 84

Follow the Flow · 86

Spicy, Spicy, Spicier · 90

Hunting or Fishing? Planning or Allowing? · · · · · · · · 92

**Part Two: How Lessons from Past Adventures
Informed and Energized My Cancer Journey · · · · · 95**

Into the Heart of Darkness* · · · · · · · · · · · · · · · · · · · 99

Just Keep Moving · 102

You Never Know Whom You Might Impact in
a Life-Changing Way · 104

Don't Try to Be Perfect · 106

A Sense of Humor Can Provide a Little Grace
and Ease · 108

Listen to Heartfelt Feedback and Adjust
Your Course · 109
Who Is on Your Team When the Stakes
Are High? · 111
Mind-Set, Mind-Set, Mind-Set · · · · · · · · · · · · · · · 113
The Virtue of Traveling Light · · · · · · · · · · · · · · · · 116
Timing Is Everything · 120
Adventure Highlights · 121
On Track or Off Track? · 124
Rafting the Grand Canyon at Flood Level · · · · · · · · 128
A Dead End or a Profound Opening? · · · · · · · · · · · 133

Part Three: The Adventure Continues · · · · · · · · 137

Acknowledgments · 145

Introduction

Everything can be taken from a man but one thing: the last of the human freedoms— to choose one's attitude in any given set of circumstances, to choose one's own way.

—*VIKTOR FRANKL,* MAN'S SEARCH FOR MEANING

This book came into being because I finally got over my resistance and reluctance to put pen to paper after the hundredth time (literally) my friends asked me when I was going to write the book about my cancer journey. So here we go…

Passport to Freedom is intended to be a sassy and sometimes humorous and irreverent look at one of life's hardest lessons. It is about how to thrive when a surprise verdict of aggressive cancer lands on your doorstep. Note I said *thrive*, not cope, live with, or survive. Our words matter, so I deliberately chose the word thrive as the meta theme for this journey, with all the ripple implications of that word.

Every book needs a storyline to create momentum and carry the reader forward. The storyline here is how I chose to make the sudden diagnosis of cancer into an adventure. Not because I am some sort of wide-eyed optimist but because that was the only way I knew how to deal with this sudden assault on my somewhat predictable life.

I have been on many adventures in my life, and some of them even resurface in this book through lessons I've learned, so I am no stranger to risk and travels. I sometimes joke that my camouflage is to look like a pretty normal, now gray-haired lady in her sixties. But underneath that exterior is a very determined, resourceful tough cookie. Also, framing this year as a bold, risky mission allowed me to tap into a different part of my personality that I call the macho jock adventurer. She had not been out to play in a while, and calling her forth has served me well on this journey.

This book is not intended to be all about me. I hope that it leaves you with insights, practical tips, and above all hope when cancer strikes you or someone you love. A dear friend and colleague recently shared with me the distinction between a motivational speaker and an inspirational speaker. At the end of a motivational talk, you are left thinking about the speaker. At the end of an inspirational talk, you are left reflecting on your own life and how to move forward using the wisdom provided. My goal is that in reading these chapters, you will be inspired to summon your own inner resources on your cancer adventure. I share my own personal story as the vehicle, because that is one place where I am an expert.

Cancer is literally an epidemic in our society right now. I wish to be a small part **of changing the conversation around cancer from one of dread, despair, and fear to one of possibility, inspired action, and resilience**. Steve Jobs spoke of "making a dent in the Universe." If I can make a small dent in the hopelessness and shock that surround a cancer diagnosis, this book will have served its purpose.

In May of 2016, after a routine yearly mammogram, I was called back and given the word that I had a particularly aggressive form of breast cancer. Now, breast cancer comes in many different flavors, and this form was one of the two major "baddies." Believe me, it was a total surprise. I had no symptoms, and I was running full speed ahead at 200 percent, building a new consulting and executive-coaching practice, which I had launched a few months previously. And then wham, the two-by-eight hit! For those not familiar with the term, a two-by-eight is a large piece of wood used in construction. Getting slammed by one is certainly not equivalent to a whisper or gentle tap on the shoulder.

Looking back, it was not a total surprise, since a couple of times previously in my life, I had used the two-by-eight method to catapult me into new adventures and phases of my life. What can I say? That is just my style, and it has served me well over the years. With hindsight, which is always 20/20, the diagnosis was just what I needed in the moment. Since I can be a little more stubborn or dense than many others, the Universe provides me with its own way of shifting and gaining momentum that I was a little slow to generate on my own.

I can now say that the cancer has been a gift, taking me to new places and on adventures in service that I did not anticipate. I might have gotten there over time on my own, but clearly there was a higher force saying, "Game on; we need you now."

Some of my readers may find the tone of this book a bit upsetting, and some will love it. The tone is very deliberate. Believe me, I am no Pollyanna when it comes to the subject of cancer; I watched several great people die of it during the year I was on my own journey. My heart goes out to their families and loved ones.

This is an adventure story in which a certain attitude is critical in opening doors to big and small miracles on the path. Today I am cancer-free, and I intend to stay that way. This book is a tribute to my team of miracle workers, who showed up in my life just when I needed them.

The format of the book is short chapters of anecdotes and stories interlaced with reflection activities, insights, and questions to ponder while you are on your own journey. And while I use cancer as a metaphor to keep the story moving, the insights also apply to any event you consider life threatening at the moment. That event could be a divorce, a car accident, or some other major life trauma that lands on your doorstep.

In today's digital world, attention spans are short. And I know from going through the rigors of chemotherapy that reading only a few pages was all I could handle at the time. So I have designed the book with that in mind. While the journey is described chronologically, you can flip to any chapter that calls to you and have fun with that short story and with what resonates with you in the moment.

Part One:
Notes from the Field on
a Yearlong Adventure

The Context: Posttraumatic Growth

Traumatic and dramatic events can be catalysts for growth. I have experienced this in both my own life and in observing the situations and evolution of others. However, I did not really focus on this while in the midst of my own year of healing and transformation. I was just "in the stew" and on the adventure. The year was almost up when posttraumatic growth—PTG—surfaced and this book started writing me. My first thought was that PTG would make a great summary and conclusion chapter for part 1 of this journey. However, Spirit had a different plan.

The basic idea behind PTG is that some people rebound and actually get stronger because of major stresses and trauma. Leveraged and nurtured properly, these events can be the catalysts for major personal growth. There can still be suffering, and the trigger circumstances are not good in themselves, but the eventual result can be transformative. The traumatic events can take many forms. Mine just happened to be cancer.

Drs. Richard Tedeshi and Lawrence Calhoun coined the term PTG in 1995 as a way to focus on the idea of growth as a potential consequence of grappling with trauma. Much of the current research on the topic is from the University of North Carolina at Charlotte. While not a new field or idea, PTG is a rapidly evolving discipline, and there are many scholarly papers available.

PTG is about rising to a new level of functioning by embracing adversity and challenges. It can be literally life changing, with no return to one's previous life and ways of relating to the world. There is often a deepening of one's spiritual connection and appreciation for life in general. Frequently, a heightened sense of focus and clearer set of priorities emerge. This growth goes beyond resilience and is about thriving and finding the benefits within the challenges. It is about a launch into a new life.

I do some of my best thinking and get some of my most powerful insights while walking our local beaches here in Virginia Beach. I stroll with my feet in the water and savor the feel of the breeze ruffling my hair. On one of these recent excursions, it became very clear that PTG was the empowering context and bigger picture for this cancer adventure. I was always choosing growth and transformation on some level, but I just didn't have the higher perspective right in the middle of the journey. Just like when you spin a kaleidoscope and all the same pieces fall into a different pattern, I had a big "aha!" when I heard about the field of PTG. I was researching it for one of my coaching clients, who experienced major growth through recovering from battle trauma, and boom! All of a sudden, it was clear that PTG is the frame for my own yearlong adventure with cancer. Just like when you decide you want a red convertible and instantly they seem to be everywhere, PTG has regularly been showing up on my radar. This book is about resilience and thriving because of a life-threatening and life-changing diagnosis. So I invite you to come along on my journey of *Passport to Freedom*.

> *A woman is like a tea bag; you never know*
> *how strong it is until it's in hot water.*
>
> —ELEANOR ROOSEVELT

Reflection, Playtime, and Continuing the Journey

Splurge and buy yourself a kaleidoscope. They come in all forms, from dime-store varieties to fancy art objects. Any kind will do. When you need to shake up your perspective and get a different look at your version of a traumatic event, give the kaleidoscope a whirl. It can be both fun and enlightening to see how many unique forms and arrangements the very same pieces can create. You can find kaleidoscope kits and even kaleidoscope glasses online. You may even want a whole collection. Have fun!

The Trigger

At the end of May 2015, I had a clear 3-D mammogram. Nothing to worry about. It was just a routine preventative healthcare measure. There has never been any cancer anyplace in my family history, and the mammogram was just a box I checked off on a yearly basis. This year was good news again, and I moved on with my life at full speed.

Then, on June 17 of the same year, about a month later, I had a near-death awareness experience (NDAE) while eating dinner at my dining room table. The next four hours were both serene and intense and shifted my life in many regards. I am pretty energy sensitive—some might even say hyperaware and hypervigilant. Sometimes that is a great thing and other times not. In more than one instance in previous adventures, that sensitivity is what kept me alive.

So that June dinner, I found myself with my head suddenly and gently on the table. I scanned my body, determined I was not having either a stroke or a heart attack, and surrendered to the experience. A bit dizzy and disoriented, I made my way to a chair a few feet away in the quiet, darkened living room, and I sat down. It was as if time had stopped and my life as I knew it stopped too. I could not have told you if I was sitting there a few minutes or for hours; the sense of timelessness, effortlessness, and oneness was profound. I could not have moved from the chair even if I had desired to do so. Emotionally, mentally, physically, and spiritually, I was totally at peace, observing myself and even humorously contemplating the experience and sensations.

In a classic near-death experience (NDE), most people are flat lining or maybe even clinically dead. There exists a great body of literature on this topic, so I will not delve too deeply into the particulars, and I will make this part brief. I chose to call this event an NDAE. I do not know how close to death I was. I do know it was very different from other out-of-body experiences I have had. I was drawn to an incredible loving light, got profound guidance from a higher source, and was given a choice in the moment to stay or to go.

Clearly, I decided to stay. It took me about four days, a couple of massages, and a Reiki session to actually get fully back into my body. (Some people will do anything to get attention!) There was no fear or pain involved at any time, just a bit of dizziness, and I was consciously present and aware the whole time. In fact, at one point during the process, I wondered with some amusement whether there is an official medical code for "soul leaving the body." Not yet, I suspect!

The booming guidance from above repeated several times and with great clarity, "If you are going to stay on the planet, you need to be willing to hold more light." Quite a concise message, and obviously, since I am writing this book, I chose to stay on good old planet Earth.

Once I finally settled back into my body, my ego went into overdrive with comments like, "I thought I was doing pretty well on this front," especially after all the time, money, and energy I have spent over the years on personal development and energy work. And in most areas of my life, I thought I was doing quite nicely, thank you very much! I felt quite successful, but clearly, it was time for a software and hardware upgrade. Simply said, God—the Source, the Universe, the Great Spirit, or whatever you choose to call it—had other plans and another view of my life.

To mark the occasion, I created a ceremony soon after the NDAE. Sailors have a ceremony—sometimes quite a raucous one—to commemorate the first time they cross the equator. I gathered a few close friends at one of our local beaches, drew a line in the sand, spoke a few hopefully inspirational words, and crossed over my line, claiming I was entering a whole new phase of my life. My new aim at that time was to be willing to hold more light. Game on! Or, as the phrase that kept coming to me soon after the NDAE would have it, "Go big or go home." That's even the title of a popular song, which I downloaded onto my computer.

Almost exactly one year later, I again had my routine 3-D mammogram, and bam, I was diagnosed with an aggressive breast cancer manifesting as two large tumors. I may never know why cancer showed up in my life then. There is no history of cancer anyplace in my family tree. Maybe it was the herbicides and pesticides I used on my llama ranch in eastern Washington, the weird diseases I contracted in my many years in Africa, or the fact that I have not been rigorous about eating organic foods. Whatever the cause, cancer showed up, and it was on a roll. It forced me to choose my adventure package from among the many options available to me.

I tend to play full out, or at least I try to. So of course my cancer would be aggressive. Was it an unconscious answer to the call to hold more light?

Some might say I created my cancer, albeit unconsciously. Others would be aghast that I would even consider this possibility. Who really knows if I did or did not? I probably will never know the answer to that question in this lifetime. What I do know is that once the cancer showed up, and I got over the tremendous initial shock, I chose to embrace the situation. For me the cancer has been an adventure and a gift, and I chose to claim it as the current answer to that call during my near-death awareness experience. So it was game on at a whole new level in ways I could never have anticipated at the time of the NDAE or the cancer diagnosis.

What I have found on this yearlong journey is that how I frame my travels and the context I create for them makes all the difference in the world and opens the field for inspiration and even miracles along the path. Sorry to be so blunt, but the bottom line is that how you embrace the shock of a diagnosis does matter. It might even be the difference between a "life sentence" of thriving and a literal death sentence. That may sound extreme to many, but that is how my choice showed up in my world at the time. It has empowered my thinking and choices and some might even say the miracles and synchronicities that have shown up.

Reflection, Playtime, and Continuing the Journey

List your personal trigger; it does not have to be related to cancer. A trigger is an act or stimulus that initiates or precipitates a chain of events.

Is it draining and depleting you, or is it renewing and energizing? If it is draining your energy mentally, emotionally, physically, or spiritually, it is time to reframe it. The dictionary definition of reframing is "changing the conceptual and/or emotional viewpoint in relation to which a situation is experienced and placing it in a different frame that fits the "facts" of a concrete situation equally well, thereby changing its entire meaning."

How can you look at the same situation in a positive way? How can it be an opportunity rather than an obstacle? List five to ten ways your trigger may be an occasion for or opening to a new perspective and even a new adventure.

Fumbling Forward Using My Intuition

When you get a cancer diagnosis, everything is a blur and overwhelming. First there is the diagnosis itself, then the testing and the appointments, and then all the information you need to sort through in short order to make potentially life-altering decisions fast. No wonder so many people just throw up their hands and say to their doctors, "Do whatever you think is best." You can certainly do what the doctor orders and follow the standard protocol for your "flavor" of breast cancer. Even that in itself can feel daunting, especially when everything feels like a rush.

The day after I got my suspicious mammogram result that required a biopsy, I was already scheduled for a cross-country trip to attend a business seminar to help grow my business. When working with my nurse care advocate to schedule the next round of testing, I asked whether I should still go on the trip. Her question back to me was, "Would you still go on the trip if you had just gotten the news you had cancer?" That was my first indication that my world was about to change in significant ways.

At first, I was very put off by her even suggesting I might have cancer. And in fact, I was quite angry that someone as seemingly healthy and as symptom-free as I was should have to stop and even consider this possibility. I was on a roll and had just spent a lot of money to move my business forward. But she was spot on. What is true is that I could not have gotten or given full value at the seminar if my mind were playing the "what-if and what-next" game. I made the decision to cancel what at that time felt like a very important trip. This is when the real journey began—ironically, with the cancellation of a trip.

Bombarded with informational binders, folders, and diagrams, with decisions on which doctors and clinics to work with, not to mention information off the Internet, it was a struggle not to feel disempowered, hopeless, and helpless. The pure shock of aggressive breast cancer felt like an assault on my whole life and way of being, not to mention my body. In a few words and in a few tests, I went from being an on-the-go, self-important consultant who was up to a big game of making a difference in the world to someone who was on a conveyor belt being poked, prodded, and told what to do.

So how did I regain my sense of self and feel as if I had some choice in all this activity? After all, this was *my* life and *my* body, and therefore I should have at least some say in what was going on.

The answer was to engage both my left-brain analytical skills and my right-brain intuitive skills. Intuition is a resource we all have and can tap into in ordinary times for creativity, and it is especially critical in times of perceived heightened danger and decision-making.

Over the years, I have been drawn to and have been more inclined to use what is now called integrative medicine to complement any care from traditional allopathic physicians. This has always worked well for me, and I have been quite healthy for my age. So my first inclination was to say no to chemotherapy for many reasons. However, my research showed that for such an aggressive form of breast cancer, HER2+, and for my stage of cancer, it could be difficult to get ahead of the power curve using only energy medicine and alternative modalities. So what to do in a time crunch to make not only one but several critical decisions? I chose to use my intuition for guidance.

Over the years, I have developed the ability to both tune in to and trust information coming to me intuitively. There are several techniques I use. And despite the fact that I really, really did not want to undertake chemotherapy, my strong guidance was to do so—and not just for me or because it was standard operating procedure. My guidance was to be a test case for integrative medicine to show the traditional medical community what could be done using this approach. And who knows, perhaps it was also to have a juicy story of my learning and adventures to share. So I chose to partake of chemotherapy despite all my emotional resistance to doing so.

That simple yet powerful act of tuning in, getting my own guidance from a higher, trusted source, and then choosing for myself shifted the whole landscape of decision-making. It gave me back my power so that I no longer felt just like another cog in the cancer machine.

From the outside, it may have looked the same as "go along to get along"—chemotherapy, followed by surgery, followed by radiation, followed by hormone therapy. More on some of those choices later. I still had the contrast CT scans, testing, and doctors' appointments, but inside I was totally transformed! I was asking questions, exploring, and making choices based on my own knowledge of what doctors and healers work with rather than blindly following orders and the often-opinionated advice of practitioners on both sides of the holistic and allopathic aisles. I took back my power and took total responsibility for my own healing. That was pivotal for the successful completion of this cancer adventure.

Reflection, Playtime, and Continuing the Journey

Sit quietly and breathe from the heart slowly and rhythmically. While breathing in this manner, focus your awareness about twelve inches above your head. What do you sense? What quiet whispers do you hear? Jot them down and repeat the process.

Buy a lovely dream journal and place it beside your bed. Each night before sleep, state a question about which you would like to receive guidance. Then see what shows up, and be sure to write it down! Often our subconscious is trying to send us messages that we are missing in our daily life, and dreams are a powerful way for us to receive the inner wisdom and counsel.

Who is the wisest person you know or admire? What would he or she do in this situation?

HOW I LEARNED NONATTACHMENT THE HARD WAY

Now I know why Buddhist monks smile and laugh all the time. It is because they are able to live from a place of nonattachment. Nonattachment is quite different from being detached, distanced, or distracted. It is more like being in the world but not of it. It is being fully present and fully participating in life in the moment while being conscious of the illusion and watching the possibilities unfold.

Right after I had what I now fondly call my two-by-eight diagnosis, I spent about two weeks wondering if the cancer had metastasized to other parts of my body. If so, that diagnosis would be a real game changer, and my choices for treatment would be very different than if the cancer were aggressive but still localized (stage two in my case).

Preliminary results indicated spots in my liver and lungs that required yet more testing, which was immediately ordered. For a variety of reasons, it took about two weeks to get the results interpreted and shared with me. Some of the initial conversations during this interval involved the "what-if" scenario, and the usual answer was one of palliative care. Translated, that means enjoy your remaining time, and we will do the best we can to keep you comfortable.

Those two weeks of uncertainty and not knowing were an amazing time of grace. My dear sister did most of the worrying for me, and it was not all fun or grace filled for her. I was left to process the "Is this the end?" question. Fortunately, because of some intensive personal growth work I had done previously, I had already said my thank-yous and had healed and completed relationships from the past, so that was not an issue. I drew up my short bucket list and was feeling very blessed that over my years of travel, I had already checked off most of the items. However, if I could only pick one of those items, I decided it would be a treehouse bed-and-breakfast tour, something I have always desired to do.

But now back to Buddha. Ironically, those two weeks of not knowing were a catalyst for an incredible moment of hanging out in the space of bliss and nonattachment. My sense was that I would either hang out here and have a great life, or I would hang out on the other side and have a great life. It was a peaceful place of grace, a win-win. And as I said when I started this chapter, it gave me a powerful insight into why Buddhist monks can remain joyous, playful, and smiling no matter what the circumstances. Those last words are the key—no matter what the circumstances. If I let the illusion, tough reality, and a sense of impending disaster dictate my internal condition, it would likely be game over. I would have been at the whim of gales and hurricane-force winds blowing through my life.

In my experience, there is a subtle but powerful difference between not caring and nonattachment. I had not given up. I was rather dancing in the place where either outcome, staying or going, was a fine and perfect next step on my soul's journey. I cannot imagine a more powerful place to stand than right there as I embraced the onslaught of the rapid decisions that seemed to be required by the test results.

I was in the midst of choosing to thrive no matter the outcome. Those two weeks gave me a glimpse of transcendence and living beyond ordinary limitations. I treasure those two weeks as a gift of what is possible in life. I wish I could say that I access that place whenever I want to do so. Sometimes I can, and sometimes I can't. And yet the sense of peace and contentment, ease and laughter remain in my system as an imprint of how truly possible it is to dance through life with a laughing Buddha.

Words Matter—Choose Them Wisely

There is a philosophy that our words create our world. This means that they impact our attitudes, our perceptions, and what many would call our personal reality. My experience of "reality" could be very different from yours depending on the language I choose, even when the circumstances appear to be the same. Imagine two people looking at and in the midst of the very same event. One might have an experience of the glass being half empty and the other of it being half full. For instance, a dear friend, trying to be empathetic, recently said to me, "You have been through hell this year."

I sat with that a few minutes and then replied, "I have been forged by fire. Watch out for this newly minted steel magnolia!"

I found distinction about language to be especially true about cancer. Most often you hear things like the "war on cancer," "keep up the fight," "combating cancer," "winning the battle," "living with cancer," "the Big C," and my least favorite, "survivor." Many find these words and metaphors helpful. For most people, the phrase "cancer survivor" is empowering because it describes their victory over a dreaded disease, which is why you hear and see the phrase so much. If these terms work for you, please use them. For me personally, it was the opposite. I was consciously choosing to thrive and transcend, not just survive. Those were the words I used and I continue to use.

My thoughts, actions, and plans became focused on how to thrive during this adventure and all the steps of treatment. In fact, I chose the term "cancer adventure" to describe this year, since that phrase allowed me to tap into some great skills and emotional resources I had used in previous parts of my life. When someone asked me what was going on, I replied, "I have cancer cells in my body," versus claiming and articulating that I had cancer. For me, this was the difference between having cancer and it having me—a subtle but all-important distinction.

As I speak and think, I pay attention to what I insert after the phrase "I am _____." Now, I am not perfect, and sometimes words like sad, tired, and nauseated certainly came out of my mouth. What I did was acknowledge that in the moment, I legitimately felt that way. The key is that I chose to briefly experience these as valid emotions or feelings but not to set up camp in that arena. I used many of the arrows in my quiver, including techniques I learned through the HeartMath^R program, and I shifted my language, attitude, and experience.

In spiritual circles, the "I am" has great power. What I put after the "I am" is what I am claiming as my truth and therefore am likely to manifest and cocreate with the Universe. I chose my words carefully and deliberately, and I encourage you to do so as well.

So for me, calling this year an adventure lifted my spirits, engaged my can-do attitude, and allowed me to draw on resources and skills from past adventures. It allowed me to plan for and participate in my travels from a place of strength and curiosity rather than depression and despair, and it propelled me into inspired action.

Reflection, Playtime, and Continuing the Journey

What words and language resonate with you? You can even make them up!

What words and phrases lift you up and give you hope on your own travels? Try them on and listen to how they feel in your body. Do they give you reassurance, comfort, and hope? Or do they feel like a heavy burden?

The license plate game[*]:

As you are driving or riding in the car, look at the license plate in front of you. Use each letter to create an "I am" statement. For example, V: I am vivacious and vibrant. For the letter U: I am unique and talented.

What delightful, juicy, and empowering "I am" phrases can you construct to lighten up the journey?

Have fun with it, and enroll your kids in this one too. It is an educational experience and can really stretch your vocabulary, just like a good game of Scrabble.

---

* *Credit goes to Unity ministers Bil and Cher Holden for this suggestion.*

Symbols Matter Too!

In the last chapter, I wrote about the importance of choosing your words carefully. Choose your metaphors and symbols wisely as well. I chose the words *thriving* and *transcending*, and I kept searching for jewelry or something I could wear to help me feel that message. I found a scarf with butterflies, symbolizing rebirth and renewal, and dragonflies, which represent transformation, but I could not find anything to my liking that represented *thrive*. There were a few items out there, but nothing really called to me.

So my dear sister, Tina, and I custom created two charm bracelets that for me captured the energy I wanted to hold and embody. I wear them proudly, and they were especially helpful to me during my four and a half months of chemotherapy.

I also created a journal of images that delighted me and called me to a wonderful future. And of course there was my collection of earrings that signaled to the world what I desired—things like dragonflies for transformation; turtles for slow, steady, and winning the race; and curvy spirals for going with the flow.

Reflection, Playtime, and Continuing the Journey

What can you create, make, or purchase that captures the positive energy of your own adventure?

Go ahead and treat yourself! Seemingly small things like this really do matter, and they send a message to the Universe. What message do you choose to send? Then wear or display the symbols where you can see them. For instance, I love dragonflies, and they are symbols of transformation. So I splurged, and I made and purchased a variety of dragonfly earrings. They make me smile and bring me delight every time I wear them.

"You Are One of Us, and We Take Care of Our Own"

WHY HAVING AN ELITE TEAM IS MISSION CRITICAL

That statement captures one of the highest compliments I have ever received. It is a part of the code of ethics for elite US Special Operations Forces and is not said casually. The second-best compliment I received was when a young Special Operations medic in our first East Coast transition institute program called me one of the best badass women he has ever met. Talk about just the right support at the right time when it was most needed!

From the time I first got the diagnosis and through the writing of this book, I have had the enormous privilege of working with Special Forces transitioning out of the military and into civilian and corporate life. There is a world-class career transition institute based in Virginia Beach and San Diego that offers a sixteen-week program serving those who have served our country so well. As a faculty member and executive coach for this program, I do the kickoff, exploring the transition process and how it relates to what the participants are going through personally, professionally, and emotionally. Then I also work with two to three program fellows per semester as their executive coach.

So what does this have to do with cancer? Just about everything. These fellows totally understand the value of mind-set and having a handpicked team you can trust with your life. They are considered elite forces for many reasons. Walking into the room of twenty-five fellows, you see that most do not look like many of the movie portrayals of them. Certainly they look like fit men, young and old, bald and with great hair, and yet on the surface, in many respects, they appear ordinary. Initially, the room appears not too different from seminars in many male-dominated industries that I have worked with around the globe. However, these men are far from ordinary. They are smart, intuitive, and able to innovate on the ground while having finely honed preparation and training for all their missions. They understand the inner game of survival and of complex, well-orchestrated missions where timing is critical. They have the ability to make quick decisions with limited information and often trust their gut on which way to go, both literally and figuratively. All these skills were also important for me, especially in my first few months of treatment.

Ninety-five percent of making it through one of the most rigorous military selection and training processes on the planet is mental focus, determination, grit, and mind-set, not brawn. So when I got my diagnosis and started treatments, I was surrounded for ten hours a week by a team that was the embodiment of those qualities. They embraced and encouraged me as I took on my own mission of choosing to thrive and not succumb to a life-threatening disease.

Working with and relying on an elite, high-performance team are critical on this cancer adventure. You can't undertake this potentially life-threatening mission without a cohesive set of individuals that you can totally trust and that you feel have your back. Sometimes the value of the skills, attitude, and group synchronization can't really be articulated. However, you can feel it, and it matters. And the longer and riskier the mission, the more it matters.

It was time to deliberately assemble my elite team, made up mostly, but not all, of powerful women. I selected a surgeon and oncologist who were supportive of me doing integrative therapies in conjunction with their specialties. Then I went about systematically and intuitively interviewing and choosing the rest of my team. I ruled out anyone on either side of the aisle—allopathic or holistic—that would not support a "yes, and" integrative approach. It is amazing how opinionated and rigid professionals from both perspectives can be when it comes to their preferred method of addressing cancer. I really wanted the "no one left behind, you are one of us, and we take care of our own" attitude that I found so comforting with my fellows at the institute.

I was blessed to find not only local resources but also energy-medicine practitioners around the country that were willing to work with me. I used healing touch, theta healing, Donna Eden energy balancing, HeartMath techniques for heart-coherence training, therapeutic essential oils, acupuncture, chiropractic adjustments, hypnotherapy meditations, nutritional counseling, and a couple of other energy-medicine modalities—all at once. I was also on several prayer lists. All of this was in addition to the standard treatment protocols for HER2+ breast cancer.

Once I reclaimed my power from the system and diagnosis, I decided I was worth the investment, and it became a liberating and fun adventure. To say that I used my default type A personality approach would be an understatement. This method was not inexpensive, but it was very, very effective. I looked at it from a return-on-investment perspective, not a cost perspective. I got great returns! Aliveness, vitality, and health are priceless. And quite frankly, without the health crisis, I probably would not have invested in myself in such an intense fashion in a concentrated period of several months. Perhaps that willingness to play full out and be an advocate for my healing and transformation were part of an answer to the call of being willing to hold more light if I was choosing to stay on the planet.

At one point, my oncologist said to me, "You are in the very top percentage of how people manage their chemotherapy—mentally, physically, and emotionally. I don't know what you are doing, but please keep doing it."

To which I replied, hopefully not too smugly, "I do know, and I will." Yahoo!

Reflection, Playtime, and Continuing the Journey

Who is on your elite team that you can trust with your life? Who can offer sound, heartfelt support on tactical decisions? On strategic choices?

"Embrace the Suck"

"Embrace the suck" is a highly technical term used by US Special Operators, and it is all about mind-set. Let's face it: chemotherapy, sitting in the chair hooked up to the IV infusion pump for hours on end, and the side effects of the treatment suck. Mentally, I understood the game, but emotionally and physically, I often wanted to bail out. I won't go graphic on the details, but to say they were often unpleasant would be an understatement.

Ironically, I never experienced any symptoms from the cancer, only from the treatments. Sometimes it feels as if the treatment is killing you more than the disease. And that would not be too far off, since chemotherapy (and there are many different protocols for the different flavors of breast cancer) is intended to indiscriminately kill off any fast-growing cells in your body. That means cancer cells, hair, and mouth and intestinal linings to name a few. So use your own imagination to picture the consequences; I will not go there with you. Given all that, mind-set was critical in order to persevere.

So what does it mean to embrace the suck? You consciously choose the path and embrace it—all of it, even the hard, messy parts—and let it fuel you as a growth opportunity. No whining allowed, or at least no more than a few minutes if you need to do so.

Sometimes growth is not pretty or pleasant in the moment. Just as elite athletes do physical training that stretches them beyond their comfort zone, endurance, and physical limitations, or a marathoner pushes through the agony of the last mile or two, chemotherapy provides the same opportunity. Let the treatment motivate you and make you stronger. Lean into it. Choose it.

During my eight hours in the chair receiving an infusion, surrounded by loving nurses, I visualized the chemicals coursing through my body as golden, healing light. Talk about a reframe! I also used my HeartMath coherence training to shift the vibration of my cells to welcome the healing and to radiate love to myself and to all those in the room with me. Crazy, hokey, enlightened—whatever you choose to call it, it worked!

Reflection, Playtime, and Continuing the Journey

For any treatment or medication you are receiving consciously, bless it and visualize it as golden light coursing through your body and cells. Feel it powerfully touching, soothing, healing, and transforming those parts of your body asking for help. Talk to your fast-growing cells with love and compassion, and ask for their help in your total healing.

*The Shake it up, baby tool**

Put on your favorite rock or dance music and move, even if only for a few minutes! Notice what happens to your energy and concerns.

---

* *Used with permission from* Toolkit for Transformation, *Suzan Thompson, PhD.*

Wigged Out, or How I Became
a Redhead Overnight

One of the hardest aspects of chemo, especially for a proud Leo woman, is losing all the hair. I had always had very thick hair and a huge Leo mane. I speak for myself but suspect that I am not alone in saying that at some point, our identity is tied to how we look and present ourselves visually in the world. Just look at all the commercials on TV and in magazines that promote that point of view.

In my journal at the time, I wrote a series of posts called "Stripped Naked I, II, and III." In my case, first it was the hair, then the eyebrows, and then the eyelashes, not to mention all the other spots where we sport hair. I had dealt with thinning eyelashes once due to an infection I picked up working overseas, and I had feared that would make me feel less attractive. Boy, did I have to confront that one and let it go!

The good news is that you get to embrace radical self-love and project your essence to the world. Are you willing and ready to be loved for who you are without all the cosmetically enhanced trappings of beauty? Sounds easy, doesn't it? However, it is not always so simple when we're constantly bombarded by the media-dictated standards of beauty. Needless to say, perspective, loving friends and family, and a good dose of humor are the best medicine.

So how does all this relate to the chapter title? As I mentioned in previous chapters, I am privileged to be a part of a career transition institute and work with about twenty-five Special Operations Forces per semester in that capacity. Working with our very first group here in Virginia Beach was smack dab in the middle of my diagnosis and intensive treatments. Often on this journey, it feels as if you are out of control. And yes, I will admit to control issues. At some point, hair is and is not one of the few things you can control. In the navy, there is a phrase: "high speed, low drag." It can refer to many things, including a particular style of haircut known as a buzz cut, in which the hair is shaved down to a fraction of an inch. Often the military uses shaving the head in boot camp as a way to help recruits leave their old identity behind in order to embrace their new one. Sound at all familiar?

Well, since I was going to lose all my hair no matter what I did, and wanting to maintain control over a few things my body was experiencing, I chose to get a buzz cut. That night I showed up in class with my new hairdo, and I got lots of high fives and comments about my courage. That made a huge difference coming from a group of fellows whose own courage in the face of danger and obstacles I totally admire. Thank you, guys! Then they circulated an e-mail among themselves, took a vote, and decided I should come in as a redhead (with a wig, of course). For the next class, I showed up as a redhead to great applause. Feeling a little outrageous in situations such as a cancer journey can be very therapeutic. Over successive classes, I was a blonde, brunette, and—everyone's favorite to this day—redhead. Adding fun, lightheartedness, and perspective made all the difference in the world.

I kept shaking it up. For my August Leo birthday, I went out to a fancy restaurant flaunting my bald, brave, bodacious-with-bling look. Baldness in men can be considered sexy, and I wanted to shake up perceptions about what is possible for women as well. For another birthday celebration, a wonderful group of women friends took me out for high tea. We wore hats, gloves, and fun jewelry, and I must say that I looked smashing in my black French beret.

Please, by all means, accept the support that is offered. Make it fun, shake it up, and be outrageous in whatever small and big ways you can in the moment. Do the planning for the trips and vacations that you have always wanted to take. One of my dear friends who now lives in Germany offered me free airfare to come visit once I was done with my treatments and could get on a plane. What a generous offer and incentive to get well! Allow that level of generosity into your life.

People really do want to be helpful and supportive; they often just do not know how. One of the things I did was to buy great cookbooks that focused on healthy eating for those in chemotherapy and dealing with cancer. I photocopied recipes that appealed to me, bought plastic freezer containers, and gave them to friends who offered their culinary skills. Having something nutritious, healing, and tasty in the freezer when I did not feel like shopping and cooking was amazing. Love comes in many forms. Please accept the love.

Reflection, Playtime, and Continuing the Journey

Take a friend and go wig shopping. Look up and try out celebrity hairstyles. Have fun, be outrageous, and experiment with a new look. The American Cancer Society has free wig boutiques. Check them out. I donated three of my five wigs to them when I again had hair. But I kept the red one!

There are also many options online. I had been resisting going gray for years, and it was trying on a gray wig that got me thinking that I actually looked pretty good that way. And voilà—here I am.

I Have Other Alligators
Closer to the Boat

I love that phrase and have borrowed it from my dear friend Susan, who grew up in Alabama. I love the visual it evokes, and it makes it very clear that in times of potential stress and overwhelming situations, I need to be very clear about my priorities. So I made a conscious choice to declare my year of treatments as an adventure and as a year of transformation. I posted a card very visibly on my dresser: "I am resilient and thriving in a year of transformation, healing, and growth." I saw it every morning when I got out of bed. And guess what I got? Just that, and often in ways I never anticipated.

In order to create that impact, I needed to release so many things in my normal routine and work life. I reprioritized my life so that I could still do the few things that really mattered to me mentally, emotionally, physically, and spiritually. It was a great exercise in values clarification, and it got me right to the core of what was important, renewing, and sustaining in my life. I made my choices matter and declared victory when I made them. It is called celebrating the small wins, and it works. At first, I could only do one thing a day, then two, and then over time even four things a day. And I did not beat myself up (most of the time) for not putting in full days. The key was that I prioritized my "alligators" and made them count. My alligators were healing and transformation. Instead of being menacing and dangerous attackers, I made them friends, companions, and even guardians during this journey.

Reflection, Playtime, and Continuing the Journey

What declarations and affirmations can you create that empower you? Where will you set them so that they act as a reminder of your commitment to yourself? The bathroom mirror and car dashboard are my favorite spots.

What are your alligators—that is, what are the priorities, people, and situations that feel scary and as if they are snapping and circling, just waiting to get you? List them in order of importance and contribution to your healing. Which ones are the most significant based on your values and dreams? How will you move forward with tiny steps to handle them even when you feel low on energy?

Synchronicity: Show Me You've Got My Back

Chemotherapy is not pleasant. Having four drugs coursing through my veins nuking every fast-growing cell in my body is not my idea of fun. One of the first questions they ask you at the beginning of every visit is, "On a scale of one to ten, how stressed are you, and what are you feeling?" They usually start with choices like angry, depressed, and hopeless and progress to sad or something equivalent. Never did I hear joyful, exhilarated, passionate, or peaceful. You get the picture.

Stress and depression are normal and logical choices given the present situation. Even with great insurance, your finances are under assault, and your financial future feels at risk. Physically, you are often depleted, exhausted, and dealing with significant side effects that make normal life feel undoable. Emotionally, you often wonder if you can keep going and continue with the journey. And spiritually, you may question if God exists, or why bad things happen to good people. Often depression is the norm, not the exception.

Fortunately, given the fact that I was using all my resilience resources, I only had two bouts of severe depression that lasted about twelve hours each. I spent many hours napping in my favorite living-room chair, contemplating my future as I nodded off, but I was severely depressed only two times.

During one of those times, I said to the Universe, "You've got to show me you have my back. I am going down here and not sure I want to stick around." And I meant it. I was really wondering what I had signed up for when I said yes to staying on the planet, an experience I described in "The Trigger."

Well, less than forty-eight hours later, I got my answer in a way I never could have anticipated or planned. Now, I am great at generating possibilities and organizing, but it took a guiding hand to orchestrate this one! One of my former HeartMath clients and a former Special Operator does surveillance and personal-protection work for global companies. He was on assignment in Malaysia, providing security for an American workshop leader who often has five thousand to ten thousand people in the room. The executive assistant to the seminar leader had the background and training to recognize what an amazing job my buddy was doing. He recognized the resilience, focus, and sustained situational awareness over long periods of time needed to do this particular job. The executive assistant approached my friend and said, "I want what you're having."

My friend said, "Call Sandy," and gave out my contact information. I got an immediate text from Malaysia, and we booked a phone consultation for his return to the States a few days later. That assistant has become one of my favorite coaching clients and a great source of warm introductions for my work.

That qualifies as a synchronicity of major proportions, just when I needed it most. It was the answer to my prayer. That story still deeply resonates with me, and I have shared it many times. It gave me hope at a critical juncture that all would be well even in the most desperate of times, and it helped me turn a corner in my treatment and attitude. It would not be too dramatic to say that synchronicity bolstered my will to go on.

Reflection, Playtime, and Continuing the Journey
The dictionary defines synchronicity as "the simultaneous occurrence of events that appear significantly related but have no discernible causal connection."

Make a list of the synchronicities occurring in your life. They may be dramatic or seemingly small, and they are all evidence that the Universe is working for you.

Here are some ideas and examples to get you started:

When I least expected it, _____ happened.

I was getting ready to make a call to a friend. Then the phone rang, and it was that very same person.

I was grappling with how to solve a difficult problem, and a book with just the right answer fell off the shelf at the bookstore.

I turned on the car radio, and a song started playing that gave me just what I needed to shift my perspective.

Giving, Receiving, and I Will Be Happy When...

CRYING IN LINE AT THE SUPERMARKET

I have always been a giver, a relatively consistent donor to causes I believe in, and a responsive ear to friends who need to talk. I prided myself on the fact that pals said I was the kind of person they felt they could call at 4:00 a.m. and I would be supportive. They never did call in the middle of the night, but they liked the idea that they could. I am blessed with an abundance of great friends and wonderful family that have each contributed to this journey in some fashion. In your darkest times, you may not feel their presence, but I bet they are there.

However, like so many of us, for much of my life, I have succumbed to the "I will be happy when" syndrome. Not all the time, but enough that it was often in the back of my consciousness, keeping me from playing full out. I'll be happy when I get the ideal job. When I lose those pesky ten pounds. When I am on my amazingly perfect vacation. When I am enjoying life with my soul mate. You get the picture. The truth is that I have had all of these at one time in my life, and I didn't allow them to make me perfectly happy. The cliché is that happiness is an inside job, and it is true. I have been happy, fulfilled, and content at times in my life, but I have not been full out outrageously happy, brimming up and spilling over, all the time on all fronts.

Having cancer cells in my body (remember what I said about word choice) allowed me to be very clear that joy and happiness are a choice. Yes, it is clichéd, and I have blithely used that phrase many times myself. I probably even have a coffee mug emblazoned with it as well. And yet now it feels different. Joy for no reason, happiness no matter what the external circumstances—they really are a choice.

In mid-September, in the midst of chemo, I was still trying to do as much for myself as I could. Asking for help was hard, since I was usually the one giving, and I usually have my radar fine-tuned to someone who needs a smile, a door opened, or a quick answer to a coaching question. Then one day, I found myself tearing up at the checkout line at the grocery store. Just walking the aisles for a few items had taken all the energy I had at the time, and I was not even sure I could get the cart and the groceries to my car. The kind woman who was bagging my groceries saw the tears running down my cheeks and offered to help me without me even asking. She got everything to the car, helped me get in, and wished me well.

So what does all of this have to do with receiving? Do you know the difference between the Sea of Galilee and the Dead Sea? The river Jordan flows into both, but one is a biological wasteland, dead, and the other is a flourishing model of rare and unique biodiversity. The difference is that the Sea of Galilee has both an inlet and an outlet. To be blunt, without a balance of giving and receiving, there can be no flow of abundance, no healing, and no thriving. It is as simple and as profound as that. One of my big lessons on this adventure is that my giving and receiving were out of whack. Period. And it took a whack on the breast, that proverbial two-by-eight, to get my attention.

Reflection, Playtime, and Continuing the Journey

Where are you out of balance? Giving too much without replenishing yourself? Over receiving without giving back of your time, talents, and treasures?

Create your own deck of colorful photos and images to spark your creativity. There are many variations on this theme, and the cards can be an excellent way to look at a situation from an entirely different perspective, lift your spirits, and get a bit wacky.

Notice and log those moments of joy, especially joy for no reason. That may feel like a real stretch, but intend that they find you and then savor them.

Divine Appointments

Even in the midst of focusing on my own healing, I had opportunities to be of service to others. One day in early September, I needed to fax some things at the local Office Depot. I could tell that the woman behind the counter was sad and that today was not one of her better days. I asked for help with the faxing and shared that while in the midst of chemo, I occasionally needed a helping hand. She then shared how she had lost both her mom and grandmother to breast cancer and that today she was feeling very lonely since she had been quite close to both of them. But when she sees an image of a dragonfly, it signals to her that her mother is present. And of course I was sporting my favorite silver dragonfly earrings!

There was no one else in the store at the time, so we spent a few minutes chatting, and I listened to her story. It is amazing how quiet, compassionate conversation can be so healing, and that is what it was for both of us, just when we both needed it. She had a smile on her face when I left the store, I had my faxing problem resolved, and we had both shared a privileged moment of deep connection. Call it a synchronicity or a divine appointment; we can all be of service no matter what is going on in our lives, and sometimes the opening comes when you least expect it.

Reflection, Playtime, and Continuing the Journey

Have you had an unexpected conversation with someone you did not know that left you both feeling better?

Have you ever smiled and said thank you to someone who appears to be having a bad day? Those are pay-it-forward moments. And sometimes when you smile, even if the other person doesn't reciprocate, you feel better too.

"Yes, and...": Lessons from Improvisational Theater

Quite a number of years ago, I lived on a sixty-acre llama ranch in eastern Washington. I commuted to consulting clients in British Columbia and Alberta, Canada, and then came home to between twenty-five and fifty llamas needing care and tending. I actually did some of my best and most innovative consulting thinking while I was fixing fences and mucking manure.

For many years, it was a wonderful, balanced lifestyle in many ways and yet isolating in others. Our ranch was about twenty miles from town, and the last couple of miles were not paved and could be pretty rough with bad weather. Neighbors were few and far between and help not always easily accessible. Many of my friends, even the locals from town, would not come out to visit, especially in the winter. I often heard them say, "You're not rural; you are remote." We had no TV or satellite for most of the years, and the Internet had not yet progressed beyond a dial-up connection. Sometimes neighbors would ride up on horseback with a DVD they had picked up in town, and we would have an impromptu beer-and-popcorn party. That was both part of the charm of the ranch and sometimes a liability.

With certain things going on in my life, consulting and designing new training programs, and with no easy access to city stimulation, I knew I needed to cultivate my creative edge. So I called a friend back in Seattle who belonged to an improv group, and I ended up hosting a weekend workshop on the ranch for about twenty friends.

In improv, a critical element is always building forward using the phrase "yes, and." You never know what the previous speaker is going to toss you. Your job is to say yes and to move the story along no matter what your critical, rational mind says. You may be thinking, "I can't do this," "It is stupid and crazy," "No one will get it," or "Where is this going?" and yet somehow it works. Everyone plays, everyone has a part, and the story unfolds in ways unimaginable at the outset. Possibilities, options, and synchronicities evolve, keeping you on the edge of your chair, and they develop a life of their own. Does that sound a bit like a cancer adventure?

When I interviewed and selected my integrative-care practitioners, I was very clear that one of my criteria was that they be willing to play with me in my healing in the "yes, and" fashion. Either/or was not what I wanted in my elite team, and I eliminated several conventional and energy-medicine healers because they were not inclined to participate in this way or to play well together.

I have mentioned in previous chapters that one great source of my strength during this yearlong adventure was to be a part of a world-class career transition institute for Special Forces. There are several things that make this group of Special Operators elite, and one of them is the "yes, and innovate on the ground" mentality. The best-scheduled and most carefully laid-out plans can go drastically south with something that seems like a minor event. The ability to regroup in the moment, recalibrate, and innovate at an almost unspoken intuitive level is often a key to their survival on missions. Cancer is a lot like that sometimes. It can take many forms, like an unexpected high fever, an unusual test result, and an allergic reaction to a medication. You are on a critical mission of restoring yourself to vital aliveness and freedom. So please try the "yes, and" approach. It will make the journey more fun, move you forward in unanticipated ways, and may even be the difference between life and death.

Reflection, Playtime, and Continuing the Journey
What is your cancer story? What ending would you like to write? What is your "yes, and" version?

How can you strengthen your "yes, and" muscle?

Check out improv groups in your city, or organize a field trip with friends to a city that has a troupe. Many towns also have MeetUp groups that get together locally to practice improv.

Compassion, Compassion, Compassion

D id I say compassion? And then throw in a big dose of self-compassion as well.

Cancer comes in many varieties, and even breast cancer has a dozen or so different flavors, each with its own protocol, procedures, and set of drug treatments. Then throw in all the cancer stages and you have a very complex mix. For breast cancer, triple negative and HER2+ are the baddies and tend to be the most aggressive. I have heard that if you start your journey in good physical shape, as I did, that is the equivalent of lowering your stage by one notch. Don't trust me on that one, though, and don't base your own treatment choices on this idea. Ask your doctor, and do your own research. But I liked the idea and tried it on for size, and for me, it was a good fit and empowering.

Everyone, especially well-meaning friends, had an opinion and advice on what I should and should not do. This was all based on anecdotal evidence and the experiences of friends with breast cancer. Who knows what stage and flavor of breast cancer they had and what their body-mind-spirit was telling them. This is where learning to trust your gut and to tune into your own intuition becomes so important. Just because something worked for someone with another form of cancer doesn't mean it is the best choice and course of action for you.

The lesson in all of this for me was to practice nonjudgment about treatments and lifestyle choices that others with cancer were making. In many instances, I would be making other choices, sometimes very different ones. Belief systems and self-talk are a significant factor, and I came to really be present to the fact others have their own adventure and soul journey, and who am I to say what is right for them? So my compassion and nonjudgment muscles kept getting exercised until I had a pretty toned set!

Having compassion for myself was sometimes a big stretch. I was used to being the go-to person with lots on my plate, and frankly, there were months during treatment when this was not possible. I had to learn not to push myself too hard and to allow myself to rest before the next treatment. This was not my normal style, and a great dose of self-compassion and self-understanding were required medicine to go along with all my integrative therapies.

The next time a friend or someone you love isn't "doing it right" by your standards, or at least the way you would do it in your "enlightened" state, please step back and add a big dose of compassion and nonjudgment to the mix. These people are truly doing the best they can in the moment with the information they can take onboard.

Notice I didn't say the information they have. Sometimes on this adventure, it is impossible to absorb and use all the input coming at you. It is their journey, and you can't travel it for them, no matter how much you would like to do so. Offer to help them when they ask, figure out fun, low-cost, low-energy things to do together to make them smile and laugh, and leave *your* judgments at home.

Reflection, Playtime, and Continuing the Journey

What fun, lighthearted movies would you enjoy? I found matinees are often best, since there are fewer people in the theater.

Ask your friends for a list of their favorite comedies, and then invite them to view them with you either at home or as an outing.

Buy a mandala coloring book and crayons and relax. Visualize and feel compassion for both yourself and others as you color or paint.

Engage Your Heart

*The longest journey you will make in your
life is from your head to your heart.*

—*Sioux proverb*

One of the significant items in my toolkit is the
HeartMath system of heartrate variability coherence training. I am a certified HeartMath trainer and
coach/mentor. I joke that I did not expect to be my own
resilience-demonstration project, but in fact, that is just
what happened. What a way to get street cred for my
executive-coaching practice and my work of changing the
conversation around cancer! It was on-the-job training at
its finest. HeartMath takes the notion of who's in charge
and looks at it from a particular perspective grounded in
science.

The messages our heart sends to our brain impact
our decision-making, capacity to connect deeply with
others, energy levels, perceptions, sleep, creativity, and
ability to manage stress. Incoherent, chaotic messages
impair our ability to function on all these levels, and
coherent, smooth waves facilitate optimum functioning.

Cancer can be stressful physically, financially, emotionally, and mentally. For me, the ability to find my center via coherence was mission critical. What does that mean? Coherence is an optimal state in which the heart, mind, and emotions are aligned and in sync, and it is a trainable skill. When one is in coherence physiologically, the immune, hormonal, and nervous systems function in a state of energetic coordination. Sounds pretty important for healing, doesn't it?

I believe getting into coherence by using the techniques daily was literally lifesaving for me, and it continues to fuel my resilience and vitality. You probably would not go a day without brushing your teeth. It is the same for me with my HeartMath practice. As of the writing of this book, I have only missed two days in close to three years.

Clearly, I was committed to this work even before my surprise diagnosis, and I continued it even in the midst of my days in chemo and other treatments. In fact, while I was hooked up to the infusion pump, I still did my sessions, and I shifted my own mental, emotional, and physiological state and radiated that to all the other patients as well. I don't know if they actually felt the difference, but I did, and the nurses certainly smiled more when I was doing it. I am into grace and ease when facing challenges, so using HeartMath tools was a standard part of my protocol. I shared with you in another chapter that my oncologist said I was dancing with chemo quite nicely. "I don't know what you are doing, but keep doing it" were her exact words.

I replied, "I *do* know what I am doing, and I will continue." HeartMath skills were and continue to be a staple of my wellness and peak-performance diet. I also used one of the tools to enhance my intuitive decision-making, which gave me new insights and comfort with the choices I was making.

Here is a bit of the scientific background for the work. The heart is the largest rhythmic source of energy in the body, even more so than the brain, and the signals it emits can be detected up to about three feet from your body. They probably extend much farther than that. Research shows that we are always broadcasting our emotional information, just like a radio station. Have you ever walked into a room and could just feel that something awful had happened there recently? Ever heard the phrase "you could have cut the tension with a knife"? Conversely, you can also feel positive vibes as well. For instance, it feels good to be around certain people, and it is not necessarily about what they say or do. We can't often articulate what we are sensing in words, but we can detect it. Our emotions can actually be measured and catalogued with a fair degree of accuracy by a magnetometer. For example, there is a different predictable signature pattern in the heart's magnetic field for appreciation than for frustration or anger. We are like a radio station that's always turned on and always broadcasting.

What is your station, dance mix or blues? What emotions are you tuned into and therefore broadcasting? What are you feeding the energy field around you? Asking that question means taking the ultimate responsibility for your own healing and your impact on friends, family, and the environment.

How does this relate to cancer? When on a cancer adventure, it is very easy to broadcast feelings of anxiety, depression, and helplessness. Yes, they are natural emotional and sometimes justifiable responses to what is happening in your life. Don't suppress the emotion, but choose to recognize and shift it as soon as you can. I make the distinction between self-awareness, identifying the emotional state, and shifting it via coherence versus what I call "setting up camp." I am going to be blunt here. In my experience, it is not helpful to set up camp or build a nice fort in the woods of depression and worry. If you broadcast "victim," that is what you will attract, and while it may get you some attention for a while, it will not contribute to your long-term healing. Often the people closest to you are also experiencing a lot of anxiety and feeling overwhelmed. Do them a favor too and be conscious of what you are broadcasting. It will allow them to be even more helpful and supportive and will reduce their stress.

I have done a lot of self-development seminars over the decades that talk about taking responsibility. They are all great workshops, and let me tell you, aggressive cancer is the ultimate test where taking responsibility is less a concept than the place where the real work and transformation happen. Consciously choosing to accept cancer as a gift, ironically, is calling me to new levels of trust and maturity for creating my world, and it all begins with engaging the heart! Please find a way to embrace your heart's wisdom. The payoff will be worth it. I promise!

> *It is only with the heart that one can see rightly; what is essential is hidden from the eyes.*
>
> —ANTOINE DE SAINT EXUPÉRY

Reflection, Playtime, and Continuing the Journey

The Quick Coherence^R Technique, used with permission from HeartMath:

Step 1: Focus your attention in the area of the heart. Imagine your breath is flowing in and out of your heart or chest area, breathing a little a slower and deeper than usual. Suggestion: Inhale five seconds and exhale five seconds, or whatever rhythm is comfortable.

Step 2: Make a sincere attempt to experience a regenerative feeling, such as appreciation or care for someone or something in your life. Suggestion: Try to re-experience the feeling you have for someone you love, a pet, a special place, an accomplishment, or focus on a feeling of calm or ease.

Further Exploration

What is your favorite radio station and why? How can you translate this into what you are choosing to broadcast? Use one of the free music services to find your favorite songs and make your own playlist. How do you feel as you are listening or singing along? Are you radiating joy and appreciation in the moment? Find your groove, and share it by broadcasting it!

What makes your heart sing? How can you do more of that activity so that you feel renewed and refreshed?

Name the emotion, write it down, and use your favorite tool to shift yourself into a more positive state.

Appreciation and gratitude help shift you into a more coherent, heartfelt state. Make it a point to articulate and even write down at least ten things you're grateful for every day. Even seemingly small things can help you build up your attitude of gratitude. I never get out of bed in the morning without saying at least five out loud to myself.

Your Why Matters!

*Those who have a "why" to live can bear
with almost any "how."*

—*Viktor E. Frankl,* Man's Search for
Meaning

Much has been written about having a life purpose and a sense of service to something greater than yourself. There are many flavors of this and many ways to get clarity on your particular mission. One of my favorite takes on this is Simon Sinek's book, *Start with Why*. His TED talk is one of the most-viewed twenty-minute talks in all their selections. He also has a new book out, *Find Your Why*.

The discovery and articulation of a personal why is also a crucial component of the curriculum at the executive- education program for transitioning Special Forces. For them, the transition to civilian life can be more intimidating than going into battle. Likewise, cancer can trigger many levels of transition both personally and professionally, some scary and some welcome. Things that used to be important no longer are, and new priorities emerge from the process of dancing with a life-threating disease. Having your personal compass and GPS can make decision-making easier, cleaner, and faster. With a real GPS, you input your destination, and it will help you calculate your route, giving you multiple options on how to get to the same end point. Having a why gives you a reason to jump out of bed every morning versus crawling out and cursing the alarm clock. Knowing and passionately living your why is the best cure for the old adage "If you don't know where you are going, anywhere will do." It is much harder to weather a transition to a new life without it! I don't know about you, but "anyplace" is not the focus of my journey, even when I am in "allowing" mode. When I am allowing, I am open to guidance but have an overall sense of where I am headed.

My why is "to clear the field for inspired action so that others can create *their ripple* in the world." The hows that support me in doing this are to access flow, embrace joy, facilitate deep connection, challenge limits, and encourage boldness. Notice that my hows are open ended and create a sense of values and direction without being restrictive and dictating specific action steps. That is where the allowing and flexibility come in.

Now, you may be asking, "What does this have to do with a journey of thriving with cancer?" Well, quite frankly, I often required a reason to drag myself out of bed in the morning, especially on those days when I really did not feel like it. Grit, resilience, and courage all come from having a deep sense of purpose. A sense of meaning and contribution larger than me helped motivate me when I most needed it. That GPS and a sense of gratitude for the blessings in my life versus focusing on how I was miserable in the moment were significant. One of my daily prayers is, "May the people and organizations I can help and have fun with find me with grace and ease." Having clarity about my why and being able to succinctly share it facilitate my service, my coaching, and my ability to say no gracefully and without guilt to the many requests I get for my time and energy. If the request is not aligned with my why, I am very comfortable declining. That saves a lot of time and effort for everyone, and it fits right in with which of my lovely alligators are demanding my attention right now.

On the cancer adventure, both effectiveness and efficiency of time, money, and energy play a role and are critical to your healing journey. Knowing your why helps you embrace the suck at some of the hardest parts of the path. So I encourage you to discover your personal why, use it as a guide, and catapult yourself into your bright, shiny, thriving new postcancer life!

Reflection, Playtime, and Continuing the Journey
Tune into your heart. What activities and people bring you joy and light you up? These are clues to your purpose and why.

Think of pivotal events in your life that have shaped you. How have they made you the person you are right now? Share these stories with trusted friends, and ask for their insights and feedback.

*Consider buying Simon Sinek's book to explore further.**

---

* *I do not receive any commissions or compensation for activities or products I recommend. I just love sharing resources that have positively impacted me on this adventure.*

What the *!@!*—You Want Me to Be Grateful?

DON'T YOU UNDERSTAND I HAVE A LIFE-THREATENING ILLNESS?

The answer to that question is an unequivocal yes, I do. Yes, you may be grappling with a life-threatening diagnosis. Yes, you may be experiencing what feels like a financial, emotional, mental, and spiritual crisis. But there are still things you can appreciate and be grateful for. How about the fact that you can take a hot shower, have indoor plumbing and clean water from the faucet, possess all your limbs, and own a cell phone for instant communication? I have lived and worked in parts of the world where none of these were a given, and every morning I bless the fact that I can take a shower and not have to walk miles for that water. I embrace the fact that I have a loving sister and friends who can drive me to treatments. I have meaningful work and volunteer opportunities that make a difference in people's lives. Stretch yourself. Even in the midst of the suck, you can find many things to be grateful for. It is all in your perspective.

Gratitude is an access point to the *now*, the deep present, where healing is possible no matter what the perceived prognosis. The emotion of appreciation coupled with heart-focused breathing is also a way to create coherence, which is a key to resilience on this journey.

In coaching, we sometimes talk about gremlins. They are the pesky creatures that sit on your shoulder and whisper things in your ear like, "You can't," "You shouldn't," and "It isn't safe." Quieting your gremlins is both important and not always easy. I used to keep quirky, funny finger puppets and give them to my clients so that when the gremlins surfaced—and they always do—they could use a little humor when working with them. The gremlins' job is to keep you safe and defend the status quo, and they take their job quite seriously. Talk to them, thank them for sharing and doing their job so well, and then move on. In cancer, there is no status quo. Gremlins can be a real liability, and it is risky to let them rule your life and decision-making. Be bold, be brave, be outrageous, and make this cancer adventure memorable. In the end, no matter what the outcomes, you will have no regrets you did.

Reflection, Playtime, and Continuing the Journey
Go online or to your favorite toy store and buy gremlin finger puppets.

What do your gremlins whisper, and how will you answer?

Celebrate the small wins. What can you appreciate about your life or about what is happening today?

Buy yourself a lovely gratitude journal, and commit to writing at least five items a day that you are grateful for and appreciate. Don't forget the seemingly mundane things that we in our affluent lifestyle often take for granted.

Set at timer, and find a place of inner peace. When the timer goes off, write in your journal, text a friend, or send a postcard to someone sharing how much he or she has contributed to your life. Make it specific. It is amazing how fast this energy comes back to you, often from unexpected sources, when you most need it.

Two Wolves

Many of you will be familiar with the fable of the two wolves. While the exact origin is uncertain, it is often referenced as a Cherokee legend. In the story, a grandfather is teaching his grandson about life. The young boy is complaining about a fight going on within him and his conflicting thoughts. The grandfather describes two wolves battling. One wolf represents sorrow, greed, and many expressions of evil. The other wolf represents joy, peace, and generosity. The grandson asks in a very concerned voice, "Which one will win?"

The grandfather replies, "Whichever one you feed."

While dancing with cancer, it can often feel as if we are at war with ourselves and our own conflicting thoughts and swirling emotions. While this is a natural part of the process, please be very mindful of which wolf are you feeding. Is it the wolf of despair, depression, and anxiety, or the wolf of possibility, hope, resilience, and thriving?

Happy Dance or Miracle?

One of the phrases I often choose is "dancing with cancer." Sometimes it is a slow, leisurely dance and sometimes an energetic jitterbug. And boy, do I love it when my surgeon does a happy dance!

The standard protocols for my version of breast cancer and stage of HER2+ are to shrink the tumors via chemotherapy, then do surgery, then radiation, and then hormone therapy for perhaps several years. A bit more on the last two options in the next chapter. I did about four and a half months of four-drug chemo, and at the end of that, I had an evaluation about whether I needed a mastectomy or a lumpectomy. Actually, the technical term for lumpectomy is partial mastectomy, but since words matter, I choose to call it a lumpectomy.

Now remember, in addition to chemo, I was doing several integrative therapies. When I had the MRI and contrast CT and went for my presurgery consult, my surgeon did an energetic happy dance! Two very significant tumors had completely disappeared, and we had the medical data to confirm it. She kept saying, "Amazing, amazing responsiveness to treatment." I love my surgeon. Besides being a very gifted doctor, she has a great sense of humor and an upbeat attitude. She always supported my integrative approach as long as it was not a replacement for conventional therapeutic options. She just smiled when I thanked her for confirming the data that my healing-touch practitioner and I had discerned a couple of days ago. Tumors disappeared, gone, nada!

The surgeon called it amazing responsiveness to treatment, but for due diligence purposes, she still needed to do what was very minor surgery. I humored her; we did a "look-see" incision to confirm, and I moved on to the next part of my adventure. I call it a miracle created with my elite team and the life force of the Universe. It is my life, my words create my world, and I get to choose what works for me.

Taking Total Responsibility

After chemo and surgery, the next anticipated step is radiation. I had formed opinions on my choices based on extensive research, and I went ahead and scheduled a consult with the radiation oncologist. He is a great guy and a very kind and empathetic person. He was very open to my questions and inquiries. My first question was, "Why would I want to radiate healthy tissues when there is no evidence of any tumors anyplace in my body?" We talked through the odds, statistical reasons, and the particulars of my personal medical profile. We kept drilling down. He appeared not to be used to patients asking so many questions, but he was quite patient and responsive. Having been married to a radiologist at one point in my life, I long ago got over seeing doctors as all-knowing gods. Experts in their field, yes, but still I focus on making informed decisions based on my own history and physiology. I am not a statistic, and my beliefs inform my decisions and my results.

In our conversation, I indicated that I would still be taking one particular drug, Herceptin, for another seven months. Herceptin is a fairly new drug, and its job is to go after all those cells in the body that have the HER+ protein on their cell membrane. It is responsible for total system cleanup! My question was, why is this insufficient? As we kept exploring, the answer was that if there were a few stray cancer cells trapped in the scar tissue from the lumpectomy, they could flare up again, and the Herceptin could not reach them. Plus there was a chance that I might need a heart stent after radiation. Sorry, but the numbers just didn't run in a way that made me comfortable. My response was, "If that is the problem, then I have other solutions based on my integrative therapies." Have you ever heard the phrase "If all you have is a hammer, then every problem looks like a nail"? I was very clear that I had a whole range of tools that could be used to address this possibility. And I continue to use them. I thanked the radiation oncologist profusely and then engaged my own set of healing protocols, now that I understood the actual issue more fully. Every situation is different, so do your homework, get full information, engage your intuition, and, with your doctor, make the choice that is appropriate for you personally. Most doctors really do have your best interest at heart, and while they have a particular expertise to offer, theirs is not the only one.

Circling back to taking total responsibility, which is the theme of this whole journey: I went back to both my surgeon and oncologist and explained my choice. I said I was going to address the reoccurrence risk in other ways but not via radiation. I even offered to sign a statement saying that I was going AMA, against medical advice, since I was taking total responsibility for my own choices. The offer was a bit of a surprise, and they declined. Both said they felt I was making an informed choice and that they would love me and continue to work with me in any case. Yes, they both used the word love! Not something you often hear in a doctor's office, and it really affirmed my choice of my elite medical team.

And then there was the hormone therapy for five years. I will make this short. I tried two drugs, got very severe side effects almost immediately, and decided not to play. I am quite comfortable assessing risks and then moving forward, and to me, the risks outweighed the rewards in both of these standard treatments. The return on investment in regard to quality of life was simply not there. I offer a huge thank-you to my doctors for respecting my choices and not trying to convince me otherwise. Yeah, team!

Now, to be very, very clear: I am not suggesting you jettison your doctor's advice, go on a squirrel hunt, and not follow well-documented treatment plans. Every situation is different, so do your homework, get full information, engage your heart and intuition, and, with your doctor, select the option that is appropriate for you personally. Most doctors really do have your best interest at heart, and while they have a particular expertise to offer, theirs is not the only one. What I am saying is be prepared to take total, absolute responsibility for your choices. No waffling allowed. Either you take responsibility or you don't. There is no going back and saying that someone else did it to you. You choose, and that is what is empowering. The multiplier effect and return on investment in that way of being in all areas of your life are huge, and they are key leverage in creating your new postcancer future!

A Labyrinth or a Maze?

Many traditional mazes are designed to be above eye level so that you cannot use line of sight to navigate your way forward. Outwardly and from a distance, both a maze and a labyrinth may have the same appearance, often made up of box-cut hedges or stone paths. However, the impact and journey of walking each is decidedly different.

With all the information, choices, and medical advice you are constantly dealing with, especially when you first get a diagnosis, life often feels as if you are walking a maze. It feels like a puzzle where there are twists, turns, and dead ends. You go in one direction, hit a wall, and have to start over again—more information and more choices.

However, walking a labyrinth is a very different experience than feeling trapped in a maze. In a labyrinth, there are no dead ends and insidious twists and turns. It is a gentle, turning, guided path into the heart of the circle. Labyrinths have been used for centuries as a tool for getting spiritual guidance. One of the most famous ones is located in the Chartres Cathedral in France, on an ancient and sacred site of access to the Divine Feminine energy revered by so many ancient cultures. We are fortunate to have a replica of this labyrinth located here in Virginia Beach at the Edgar Cayce Foundation, more formally called the Association for Research and Enlightenment. You get a view of the Atlantic Ocean, listen to a sparkling fountain, appreciate wonderful gardens, and walk the labyrinth at the same time. What a blessing to have this available locally.

You can walk the guided path for pure pleasure as a walking mediation, and you can also use it as a tool for gaining insight and guidance for pressing issues. Pose a question as you walk slowly inward, and activate your deep listening and connecting skills. Once in the center, salute the four directions in traditional Native American style and then tune in even more intently, asking for wisdom related to the question you have posed. Don't censor the information and gentle whispers. Truly open yourself up to whatever the Universe wants you to hear as its gift in the moment. Then journey outward into the world with your message via the same path that took you on your inward journey.

A couple of times I walked this labyrinth with a supportive friend, and we compared notes after our contemplative journey. We then also explored ways to mutually support each other, which facilitated deep sharing and connection. In those moments when I was in need of a refresh, a reset, and a reframe, I often used walking the labyrinth as a tool for getting a higher perspective on my adventure. Whether you are actively seeking a way forward or want to reclaim some peace and comfort on the cancer journey, I highly recommend walking the labyrinth on a regular basis.

Reflection, Playtime, and Continuing the Journey
Most cities will have a labyrinth open to the public that you can access and walk. The Internet will be able to help you locate something close to you. Consider taking a friend and a picnic lunch and make it an outing.

Find some paving stones and lay out a labyrinth pattern in your backyard. You can even make it a family project. It does not have to be fancy. There are even cloth versions you can lay out temporarily in a big open space. Then whenever you need to find calm, quiet your soul, or get guidance, take a meditative stroll and be open to shifts, renewal, and subtle information.

Service as Healing

Even in the midst of my most trying periods, I continued to volunteer ten to twelve hours a week. I did this not out of altruism but because of the input and benefit to me. This was in addition to keeping up coaching with my existing clients. You may not be able to do much because of the lack of physical energy. However, something as simple as a warm smile and a thank-you to someone as he or she opens the door for you can transform someone else's life. Check out the chapter "Divine Appointments" for an example.

As I continued to show up in service at the transition institute for Special Forces, I received more from the fellows and staff than I gave. I was truly honored to serve those who have given so much. Showing up two nights a week, except on my actual chemo days, gave me a structure, a sense of purpose, lots of great hugs, and the ability to hang out in an environment with those who have demonstrated again and again that mind-set is everything.

When people asked me how I was doing, I said, "I am getting better and better and sassier and sassier every day." Or as I listened to the trauma and drama in others' lives, I often commented to myself and sometimes even out loud, "Thank you very much. I will take my own life and challenges over theirs." It is all in the perspective. And it is a way to affirm that no matter what the current situation, I am empowered by the choices I make, and quite frankly, I have so much to be grateful for.

You too can feel this way. Declare yourself a no-victim zone. No kidding. It will make a difference in your life and attitude and for those around you. Small acts of kindness have a multiplier impact, just like the butterfly effect, and can improve your life in ways that mysteriously unfold over time. Try it out and notice what happens!

Reflection, Playtime, and Continuing the Journey
Commit to small acts of service, just for fun, and notice what happens. Remember the pay-it-forward suggestion. Experiment and try out a few different things. For instance, pay for the coffee for the next person in line, or put money in an about-to-expire parking meter. Then notice how this makes you feel.

Make a list of how you can show love and appreciation for those around you. Flowers, a card, or a text. It does not have to be expensive. Then, à la Nike, just do it.

I Am Human Too!

Sometimes I get tired of feeling brave and having to act like a role model. At times, it just plain sucks. That about says it all. On any journey, there are ups and downs and times when you wonder why you started on this path in the first place. (It seemed like a good idea at the time...) Sometimes at the most arduous points during chemo, I just wanted to be hugged, comforted, and told everything was going to be OK. I wanted to be told that I would meet my soul mate, enjoy a newly prosperous life, and all my dreams would come true. But despite loving intentions, no one around me could offer those guarantees.

I expected myself to be brave, and that is how most people interact with me as well. I can be prone to stomping my feet and declaring I want a breakthrough now! And by the way, I want the breakthrough without having to endure the breakdown process to get there. How do you think the caterpillar feels as it dissolves into the gelatinous goo called imaginal cells inside its cocoon? Does it know or envision becoming a beautiful, transcendent butterfly? I suspect not. Its deep *now* in the present moment is disintegration.

What to do? How can I both be brave and give myself the space to be with my emotions too? I can just love them, let them flow through without being attached to them, and not encourage them to set up permanent camp. One of the tricks I use is to give myself permission to be as sad or depressed as I can for ten minutes. I really go for it and play full out. Usually I find I can't even last the full ten minutes. If I do, then I give myself another ten, go deeper, and get more fully self-expressed with that particular emotion. And then I use my HeartMath techniques and other tools to get back in sync and on track.

On some of my longer trips and adventure travels, sometimes all I can do is continue to move forward. Sometimes it is slow progress, but you don't want to get off the roller coaster in the middle of the ride. You don't stop halfway across the Sahara and give up because you are tired, and you certainly can't get off in the middle of the Colorado River when you're rafting the Grand Canyon at flood level.

Embrace the ride, acknowledge the suck, have some compassion for yourself, and keep trucking. Doing so will build up that choice muscle, and it will serve you well in the end.

Reflection, Playtime, and Continuing the Journey
To help shift your energy, buy a journal and start writing—just for you. Collect inspirational photos, images, poems, and cards, and when you are feeling very "human," let this special book lift your spirits and mood.

Curing, Healing, and Survivor's Guilt

One of the insights that was really reinforced for me on this adventure is the distinction between healing and curing. In the process of dancing with cancer, it is possible to be healed of many old emotional wounds and past traumas and yet still succumb to the physical impact of the disease. Depending on your spiritual and religious belief systems, the result can still be an enormous blessing. I have heard of families reunited and latent love expressed as someone is in the final stages of his or her transition. That is a healing and can occur in many forms and on many levels. And then there is the cure, when all visible traces of the disease are no longer detectable in the body, even with the most sensitive instruments and rigorous testing.

Now, in my own personal belief system, it is possible to be cured but not healed. The classic medical benchmark is five years cancer-free. I am not sure what the actual statistics are for reoccurrence, but historically, the likelihood can be high, depending on the form of cancer. This means there is also the whole conversation about living with cancer—that is, having no "cure." My oncologist's office had books on that topic. But the same relationship issues keep surfacing, the same conflicts and arguments regenerate, and the lack of self-love continues to contribute to a variety of physical and emotional addictions or symptoms totally unrelated to the cancer, and it makes me wonder…

Obviously, the most powerful combination is both healing and curing. That is why I embraced so many integrative healing modalities all at once. Call me a classic overachiever, because I am. I chose to use this yearlong adventure as a powerful opening to do as much clearing, completing, and energy balancing as I could fit in!

Part of the reason I call it my cancer adventure is that I invested heavily in myself to explore the dis-ease of cancer on all levels—mentally, spiritually, emotionally, and physically. And by the way, *dis-ease* is not a typo. Casting the word this way takes the energy out of the diagnosis. If it is a matter of not being at ease with something in my life, I have tools, techniques, and a team to address that state. In my role as a consultant, I look at return on investment for time, money, and energy, and the ROI on my healing modalities was enormous. And that investment is still reverberating, not just in the "all clear" but also as a catapult into my next adventure.

And there is the issue of survivor's guilt. During my year of healing and transformation, I personally watched several good people with loving families die from cancer. Sometimes I was hit with guilt about why I was still here. Why am I still not only standing but also thriving? I can't give you a good answer to that, and it would be presumptuous to even try. All I can say, yet again, is to have compassion for each individual's soul journey.

It is hard to watch, let alone be a part of, the loss of someone near and dear to you, especially if you go into "woulda, coulda, shoulda" mode. Viewing it as a soul journey at least gave me some peace and perspective for others and myself as I observed their healing and curing path.

Are You Waiting for the Other Shoe to Drop?

C onsciously or unconsciously, it is easy to buy into the classic medical milestones. Five years cancer-free… ten years…pick your milestone. They are statistically valid and based on large sets of data. I mentioned in a previous chapter that I chose not to be a statistic. I also chose not to use the word remission. To me, remission implies that cancer might come back. Instead I say that I am free and clear of having cancer cells in my body in this moment.

There is a motivational poster often seen in offices with the phrase "Your attitude determines your altitude." I chose to fly high and create my own numbers and statistical evidence. We, my team and I, did that in making the tumors disappear, so why not everything else about the disease as well? How happy can I be? How joyous? What are the metrics for that?

Reflection, Playtime, and Continuing the Journey
What is your favorite shoe style? Do you favor comfortable, practical flats or sexy, bold stilettos? Go to a shoe store, or have fun shopping online. Try on outrageous shoes you might

never see yourself wearing in your "normal" life. You don't have to actually buy them. The point is to play outside your comfort zone, even for a few minutes. What shoes fit with your next adventure?

Buy a magic wand (I have several) and wave it. What would fulfillment look and feel like in your postcancer life? This is about dreaming big and sharing your dreams and desires with the Universe. Please notice I did not mention success or focusing on how the dreams might manifest. Write down the qualities and characteristics of those desires, and then let the Universe go to work on your behalf!

Follow the Flow

I have savored Steven Kotler's book *The Rise of Superman**
and his most recent book, *Stealing Fire*,* with his coau-
thor, Jamie Wheal. One of the most compelling stories for
me on this adventure was how Steven healed himself from
totally debilitating Lyme disease by being in the flow. He
had literally been bedridden for almost three years and
had tried everything that conventional medicine had to
offer, with no sustainable results. He felt pretty hopeless
and depressed. Then one day, some of his friends picked
him up and forced him to go surfing. Muscle memory
from previously being a surfer kicked in, and in that brief
altered state called flow, he got a glimpse of what was possible. It took him three weeks to recover the first time, but
he got on his board again and again. He kept accessing
that flow state via surfing, and today he is a best-selling
author. Please Google him for a longer, more detailed version of this story.

The book *Stealing Fire* resonated with me on many
levels, including my own experiences of flow individu-
ally and being in the flow state with a high-performing
group. Intending to add another tool to my toolkit, I
registered for the Flow Genome online course*. I can

honestly say it is one of the best online courses I have ever taken. I enrolled at about the halfway mark in my yearlong adventure, and it was the perfect opportunity at the perfect time. Yes, it contributed to my own healing. And I am an advocate of the creativity, insights, resilience, and peak performance accessible in the flow state. I was already doing many of the practices suggested, including my heartrate variability coherence training using HeartMath tools and feedback techniques. The Flow Genome course also gave me a structure and interactive community and lots of insights to help me keep my healing momentum.

The characteristics of the flow state include a sense of selflessness, timelessness, effortlessness, and richness of experience. I tuned my radar to not only how to trigger flow states for myself but to discover how others experience it as well. I informally interviewed musicians and an artist who is a cancer thriver himself and who facilitates and creates an environment where his students can tap into flow. And it's no coincidence that one of the women I spoke to in the studio described in almost the same exact words used in *Stealing Fire* her own experience of flow and its healing impact on her cancer travels. In our short conversation, the few comments I made touched her deeply, and she said that was exactly what she needed to hear in that moment. Score another win for synchronicity and divine appointments! I have no memory of what I actually said. It was one of those times I fondly call "drop and deliver," when a higher force was using me as a vehicle for healing.

Mihaly Csikszentmihalyi, the grandfather of flow studies, discovered that the happiest people are those that can access the flow state. Some use sports, some art or music, and some writing and even coding. We all have our own preferences and on-ramps to flow.

Being able to consistently access flow can be a great gift in a life-threatening situation. Remember Steven's story and figure out your own approach. I invite you to use the flow state as a springboard to a more fulfilling life. The ripple effect is enormous, and you can emerge from this seemingly perilous adventure with access to grander vistas and higher mountains than were possible before you began. Follow your flow. It is enriching, healing, and the only real way to solve the "wicked problems" you and our world are facing.

I do not receive any commissions or compensation for activities or products I recommend. I just love sharing resources that have positively impacted me on this adventure.

Reflection, Playtime, and Continuing the Journey
Choose your flow flavors, and give it a go! Incorporate them into your daily life. Experiment and find your favorites. Here are some starting ideas:

- *Improvisational theater*
- *Music, both playing and listening*

- *Writing*
- *Coding*
- *Action sports*
- *Walking in peaceful outdoor environments*

Spicy, Spicy, Spicier

AM I BEING OUTRAGEOUS YET?

In chemo, you lose your sense of taste, and food feels like a burden and a nutritional chore rather than a sensual pleasure. One of the hot tips given to me by a fellow traveler was to keep an extensive journal of medications, side effects, and the few days between treatments when I could actually taste anything. The idea is that you save your favorite meals for those days when there was at least a chance of enjoying them. That was great advice, and I followed it. It grounded me and gave me helpful insights into predictable patterns that I was experiencing, especially while in chemotherapy.

What I found was that I could taste spicy foods and sugar-filled ones. Now, sugar is rocket fuel for fast-growing cancer cells, but sometimes you gotta do what you gotta do just to get something down. Fresh fruits and vegetables, my previous staples, did not work with a digestive system under assault. So spicy was good, and I forgave myself for the times I succumbed to the temptations and allure of sugar. On a side note, about nine months into the journey, I got "fresh" again and cut all sugar- and flour-based products out of my diet. I feel so much better, and my blood-sugar levels, out of control from the medications, came back to normal. On the days I could eat, spicy cooked sushi became one of my favorites.

How can you be spicy and outrageous in both your food and activities? Rich, novel environments can help trigger the flow state, which is also beneficial for healing. Don't do anything stupid. Assess your risks, but go for the gusto in whatever way you can. Rattle a few cages; ruffle a few feathers so that you can feel the breeze in your hair. I promise it will make a difference. Especially on this particular journey, we all need to nurture our sense of aliveness and possibility.

> *Don't ask what the world needs. Ask what makes you come alive, and go do it. Because what the world needs is people who have come alive.*
>
> —*HOWARD THURMAN*

Hunting or Fishing?
Planning or Allowing?

I am a fairly well-organized, logical thinker and planner as well as a pretty intuitive visionary. I even mention these skills on one of my websites. Utilizing those abilities is a significant part of what has made me successful in my career as an international coach, consultant, and trainer.

One of my biggest lessons, which I continue to learn, is how to fish and allow. Hunting implies tracking and going after the intended big game, with plans and PERT (program evaluation review technique) charts used to schedule, organize, and coordinate project tasks. It is still often my default setting as I work to manifest things I desire in my life. Fishing is quieter and lets juicy morsels come to you rather than your having to scout for and pursue them. Yes, you still need to experiment to find the right bait, but that is part of the fun. When I am allowing, it is just like the stories in the "Synchronicity: Show Me You've Got My Back" and "Divine Appointments" chapters. It is about the now and asking in this present moment, "What one thing can I do that will support me and move me forward?" There is a sense of ease, grace, and effortlessness. Synchronicities abound and ideas flow.

People, connections, and even unanticipated sources of income show up out of nowhere. Surprise and delight become regular occurrences.

In fact, writing this book is an exercise in allowing. Once I actually shared that I was willing to put pen to paper, people, out of their enthusiastic support, kept asking questions like, "How long will it be?" "Who is the target audience?" "Will you do workshops?" "Who is the publisher?" "How will you leverage it?" "When will it be ready?" The answer to all those questions at this stage is, "I don't know, and I am totally comfortable with not knowing." I am just enjoying the process and trusting that these words and my story will impact those it needs to reach in a positive way, coming as it does from my intention to transform the conversation around breast cancer from one of dread, despair, and fear to one of possibility, inspired action, and resilience.

Surrender is not always easy, and I acknowledge that it is still one of my biggest lessons from this adventure. I am unlearning over sixty years of successful habits, and that takes time and patience. But it is a case of "you can't get there from here" to launch into the next phase of my life adventures with the wisdom gleaned from this year of travels. My advice to both myself and to you is to feel into and trust the allowing. The Universe really does have your back if you give it room to play without micromanaging the outcome.

Part Two:
How Lessons from Past
Adventures Informed
and Energized My
Cancer Journey

I have been very blessed to live a multifaceted life full of big and small adventures. I spent more than five years in Africa, the first three as a Peace Corps volunteer in the Congo, then travelling for a year, and then working in countries such as the Ivory Coast and Sudan. In addition, I spent almost a year "commuting" to South Africa from Virginia Beach. I have chased solar eclipses in Mazatlán, worked on the luscious island of Sri Lanka, and lived and traveled in Europe. My dad and I have hiked New Zealand and Costa Rica together. I have run a sixty-acre llama ranch in eastern Washington while consulting in Canada, and I have been married twice. I have been on amazing camping trips and have hiked and climbed all over the country, and along the way, I have learned from all these travels. Sometimes I learned the easy way and sometimes the hard way. Remember the section on post-traumatic growth and the two-by-eight metaphor? Well, that shoe still fits!

For part 2 of *Passport to Freedom*, I have selected just a few of these experiences that have the most bearing on the cancer adventure. Some of the rest of the treks may show up in a future book. Recall that I chose to frame the cancer diagnosis as an adventure to propel me on the year of treatments and healing. That is what I know how to do: make life an adventure. And that framing allowed me to draw from my past safaris in a powerful way.

What is true for me, and I suspect for most of us, is that we are shaped, seasoned, and honed by the events in our lives and our choices around them. We can either get stuck in our stories and tolerate the status quo or allow ourselves to be forged by fire like a finely tempered sword or steel magnolia. So while this is a brief exploration of some of my life, I would also ask you to reflect on the experiences that have made you the amazing person you are right now! Let's begin the journey...

> *Security is mostly a superstition. It does not exist in nature, nor do the children of men as a whole experience it. Avoiding danger is no safer in the long run than outright exposure. Life is either a daring adventure, or nothing.*
>
> —HELEN KELLER

Into the Heart of Darkness[*]

MY YEARS IN THE CONGO

MY YEARS IN THE CONGO

From 1974 to 1977, I spent three years in the Democratic Republic of the Congo (DRC), then called Zaire, as a Peace Corps volunteer (PCV). I taught high school science for two years and then extended my stay for a third year to do public-health research. The Peace Corps recruitment slogan at the time was "The toughest job you will ever love." Now it is "The world is calling. How far will you go?" Both taglines are powerfully true. In fact, I almost headed out to Mongolia for a second round of volunteering just before the cancer hit.

I left a high-pressure, promising academic career (I was enrolled in a PhD program at Yale) and headed off to Africa to fulfill my childhood Jane Goodall fantasy. That is not as outrageous as it sounds. I was very blessed to meet her while a graduate student at Yale and have only the utmost respect and admiration for her work in the world and for her as a person. She was and still is a role model for me.

Instead of doing animal-behavior research under the Smithsonian and Peace Corps umbrella, which was the original plan, and consistent with my educational background, I ended up in the Congo teaching high school biology and chemistry. Someone at Peace Corps headquarters apparently figured out that I spoke passable French from having spent a summer in Switzerland, and science teachers were desperately needed in the DRC. Faced with a choice and a huge dilemma over what at first felt like a bait and switch, I still decided to go.

Don't back down from your dreams despite the surprises and big forks in the road. Check in, see if the new opportunity "has heart," and if so, embrace the new adventure and see where it goes. Sounds a bit like the two-by-eight and handling the cancer option.

I served in a bush school for two years, teaching under very primitive conditions. And then I spent a third year doing public-health research at the main government hospital in the capital, Kinshasa. There I weathered the first-ever outbreak of Ebola when it hit the hospitals in Kinshasa. There are many stories from those three years, but they are not for this book—maybe another one.

It used to bother me when I got back to the States and people would ask me to summarize three years of extraordinary adventures and ups and downs in the Congo plus a year of travel. They wanted it in twenty-five words or less. Friends, family, and acquaintances were genuinely curious but had no context for my stories. That is why when Peace Corps volunteers, like old war buddies, get together over a beer, we swap stories. It doesn't matter where you served; at least you are talking to someone who understands.

How does this relate to the cancer adventure? Unless someone has been through it, has experienced the emotions, physical tests and trials, and the thrill of seemingly small victories, he or she can never really empathize with your voyage. Please cut them some slack. Have some compassion. At least they are trying to understand and be supportive.

What follows is a Cliff Notes version of my lessons from the field and how they informed this year of travels.

---

* The title of this chapter is taken from Joseph Conrad's novel of the same name. Please note, however, that my experience of living and working in the Congo was not one of darkness but of connection, courage, passion, and incredible joy under the most difficult of conditions.

Just Keep Moving

Sometimes you just need to keep focused on the next milestone and keep moving. Many of those in Special Forces I have been privileged to work with say that is how they made it through the most grueling military selection process on the planet. As in, "I will focus on making it to lunch, and then I can decide if I will quit." And they don't quit. Then the focus shifts to making it to dinner and then on to breakfast. It is called segmentation. Break down what appears to be overwhelming into bite-size morsels and then bite them off one by one.

During my first year as a PCV, my version of segmentation was crossing the days off in half-day segments. That is the only time in my life I have done that—and it worked. The Congo, like the military selection process above, has a very high initial dropout rate. It was a particularly tough posting for many reasons in addition to the normal cross-cultural adaptation. I later learned that the Peace Corps doctor, when he did his site visit, reported that he didn't think I would make it through the year. The Congo is a tough country and still is, and at that time, it had one of the highest overall PCV attrition rates of any country. As I have said before, mind-set is everything, and once I learned the ropes and got my head in this new game, I actually extended my service for a third year. Even in the middle of that tumultuous first year, there were moments of deep connection, courage, joy, and pleasure in small things. That is where I kept my focus and went on half day by half day.

Cancer can be a bit like that too. It certainly is a game changer. Keep focused on the next milestone, and they all add up. It can be the next birthday or holiday, the great results from an exam, the countdown on the treatments. Celebrate the small wins, and keep moving toward your goal.

Being a PCV was exceptional training in grit and resilience and my first real test of endurance. I was able to use this learning and perspective for my yearlong cancer adventure. Any growth experience will stretch us, often to our perceived limits. During these times, we learn to dig deep into our center of resourcefulness and not only survive but also thrive. By the way, I mastered the grit part and, as mentioned, extended my stay for a third year. You too can call forth this same energy on your adventures.

Life begins at the edge of your comfort zone.

—*Neal Donald Walsh*

You Never Know Whom You Might Impact in a Life-Changing Way

More than a decade after being a PCV and my subsequent travels, I was living and working in Seattle and feeling a bit depressed, as can happen to me if I haven't seen the sun for months. I was walking up to my local Starbucks on a Saturday morning, mumbling some variation on "I wonder if I have ever made a difference in this world?" Mentally and intellectually, I knew I had, but at that particular moment, I just wasn't feeling it. Then a whopper synchronicity struck just when I least expected it and needed it most. I got my coffee, wandered home, and received a phone call. It was one of my former students from that first year of teaching in the bush in the Congo. He had spent almost two years trying to track me down. Remember, that was in the mid-'80s, without all our current Internet connections. He had called just to say thank you. At that time, he was working as a World Bank official in Washington, DC. He had gone from a bush school to one of the most prestigious organizations in the world. His call gave me the perfect answer to the question I had been mulling. Talk about possibility and perseverance! I share this not to toot my own horn but to illustrate how being of service can have a ripple effect of extraordinary magnitude. Many other PCVs can share similar stories.

Reflection, Playtime, and Continuing the Journey
Whom can you impact by your choices of how you deal with and dance with cancer?

> *I've learned that people will forget what you said, people will forget what you did, but people will never forget how you made them feel.*
>
> —*MAYA ANGELOU*

Don't Try to Be Perfect

You can't be everything to everyone all the time. Get over even trying!

I invite you to move through your adventure with the intention to thrive. I know I am being redundant, but I am doing so deliberately. I taught high school biology and science in French without textbooks or lab equipment, and at times, I even had to scrounge for chalk. Ultimately, I created my own version of a textbook from some references I had brought with me in my sixty pounds of allotted luggage. I then translated those references into French, and my students put the lessons on the blackboard and copied them down in their tablets during their break and lunch hour. Talk about innovating on the ground!

Do the best you can, and keep moving! I had to teach to a national exam even under those circumstances. What kept me going was the thought that I was training future doctors and nurses in a country that desperately needed help, and I knew if I didn't show up, they were not going to get their basic science instruction. That was a first glimpse for me of the power of a personal why. And the students, sometimes seventeen to nineteen years old due to school disruptions from war, mirrored my commitment. They too excelled.

So, back to not being perfect. While I had a pretty extensive French vocabulary, my students used to tease me that my grammar was quite creative. They would laugh and then gently correct me. Often I made up a "Frenchified" version of a technical scientific term, gave the explanation, and made it part of their homework to do further research. Accepting imperfection became part of our bonding experience.

You will experience ups and downs on a cancer adventure. You will have moments of comfort and peace and moments of extreme stretching and wondering if you can even continue. Don't try to be perfect. You don't need to be brave every moment you breathe. The overall trajectory and mind-set matter and will shape your healing outcomes. Just keep choosing and trekking.

A Sense of Humor Can Provide
a Little Grace and Ease

Then there is the story of the disappearing pencils. In the Congo, pencils were very hard to come by and a prized commodity for many reasons. Bic pens were considered an even greater treasure. You can see now why I can be grateful for even small things we take for granted. My students were convinced that I had magic pencils that always gave the right answers. At first, I was very annoyed when they kept mysteriously disappearing. That shifted to amusement, and then I made a point of stocking up on them on my vacation visits to the city, where I could get school supplies. Eventually, I just considered it a contribution to the local economy. Who knows, maybe those pencils did contain all the answers!

Don't sweat the small stuff. There is plenty of big stuff to manage on your trip. Save your energy and focus for mission-critical items and events. In the next chapter, I share some dream sequences about letting go of baggage in order to travel lightly.

Reflection, Playtime, and Continuing the Journey
What can you treat lightly, irreverently, and with a dose of humor when everything seems bleak and heavy?

Listen to Heartfelt Feedback and Adjust Your Course

I tend to be a pretty direct problem solver. Give me an issue, and I will use every resource at my disposal to come up with a solution. But life doesn't always work that way. One of my first big aha moments in my first year as a PCV in the Congo was some gentle feedback I got during the initial week at my first school. I was being my usual self in a staff meeting, and one of the older Congolese teachers, who was also a neighbor and who became a good friend, took me aside and said, "Sandy, that is not the way we do it around here." He continued, "Sometimes we just need to talk around things for a while before we try to address the problem." That was some of the best advice I have ever been given, and it has served me well over time, both working cross-culturally and in my consulting and coaching. Call it situational leadership or sensitivity; paying attention to cultural norms will get you a lot farther and with a smoother ride. That gentle, well-intentioned advice contributed to my success and three amazing years in the one of the "toughest jobs you will ever love."

How does this apply to a cancer adventure? In addition to trusting your own intuition, are you willing to listen to an outside perspective that may make you more successful on your trip? A great piece of counsel I was offered was to get adequate food and nutrition in order to support my journey. I listened, and after some research, I found a high-grade protein powder that I could not only keep down but also enjoy. That advice made all the difference in the world and helped combat the muscle loss that can accompany treatment. I watched too many fellow travelers in chemo succumb to Starbucks Frappuccinos as standard fare. Many things taste good in the moment but are not good provisions for the longer trek to wellness.

Reflection, Playtime, and Continuing the Journey

Whom do you trust to give you advice and a supportive perspective? Will you actually listen and implement the suggestions or input? Are you willing to experiment and try the new ideas on for size, knowing that you can always discard them if they don't fit?

Who Is on Your Team When the Stakes Are High?

This was a fundamental lesson I learned in the Congo that fast-forwarded into the present adventure. You might call this story a prequel to a chapter in part 1.

My first year in the Congo, then president Mobutu claimed the CIA had plotted a coup to depose him. He announced on the radio, "No American will make it out of the country alive." Who knows what the CIA really planned or plotted, but that threat had me and my postmates take a hard look at our remote situation. We were in the bush, and even in the best of circumstances, getting out of the country would have been hard, expensive, and problematic. Now, that happened close to forty-five years ago, and I still remember the impact. I recall wondering who would be willing to put themselves at risk to shelter us if the need arose. Fortunately, we did not have to activate the plan. The deep relationships and shared mission with our fellow Congolese teachers and certain community members gave me the confidence that we could weather the storm.

Be deliberate about cultivating your trusted team. You never know when they will make the difference in a critical situation. Take the time to enjoy, connect, and cultivate deep relationships. Build the emotional bank account. You never know when you might need their support, rides, and hugs as you embrace your cancer adventure.

Mind-Set, Mind-Set, Mind-Set

This was my first introduction to the fact that although sometimes the threat is scary from the outside, it is how you manage yourself internally that really counts. During my third year in the Congo, I was stationed in the capital, Kinshasa, doing public-health research at the main government hospital, then called Mama Yemo after President Mobutu's mother. In a third-world hospital, a dedicated staff is always trying to manage overwhelming health problems with very limited resources.

It was 1977, and a strange hemorrhagic disease started showing up in the northern provinces and killing better than 90 percent of those who contracted it. At that time, since this was the first known epidemic, no one knew how it was transmitted. Was it airborne? Did it require direct contact with the infected? Patients started showing up and dying in the Kinshasa hospitals even though the epicenter of the disease was more than one thousand miles away. Most of them came down by riverboat and were dying by the time they reached the capital. Then health-care workers started dying too.

The Centers for Disease Control (CDC) sent in teams of scientists and doctors. The whole country was put on quarantine and lockdown—or at least that was the intention. As PCVs, we could not have gotten on a plane to flee even if we had wanted to. The Peace Corps pulled all its volunteers out of the hospitals and ordered us not to leave our compound. One volunteer up north, a lab tech, pricked his finger with an infected needle. They flew in an isolation chamber, sealed him up, and flew him to a containment center in South Africa. They were able to get enough blood serum from the very few survivors and gave it to him, and he survived. It all felt surreal, like the movie *Outbreak*. To this day, I have no memory of how we handled the basics and got food, since we were forbidden to go to the stores or market.

Eventually the CDC was able to determine that the disease spread by direct contact with the body fluids of an infected person and that the rapid spread up north was due to some of the burial practices that necessitated handling the bodies. This turned out to be critical information for later Ebola outbreaks.

The key to surviving in this instance, both emotionally and physically, despite the perceived terror, was to cultivate a powerful mind-set. We had a bigger team in place geared up to handle the unknown. Through methodical action and extraordinary courage, they got the situation under control. Having an integrated team during my cancer adventure was a lot like knowing the CDC had us covered no matter what. In part 1 I emphasized the

importance of having a great team that encourages a resilient and courageous mind-set no matter what the appear-
ances. Find a way to quiet the fear. And most of all trust
that the Universe has your back no matter what it may
look like in the moment.

The Virtue of Traveling Light

LESSONS FROM THE SAHARA

For this book I have consciously used the metaphor of an adventure trip or a journey. It is a very practical, apropos metaphor, and it is something that has been an integral part of my life—travel, adventure, trips—and I know you have your own version of this, although the form may not look like mine.

In a previous chapter, I mentioned that my camouflage is looking like a normal, slightly rounded, now-gray-haired lady of a certain age. All that is true. In my younger years, my "macho jock adventuress" had full rein in running my life—and was having a great time, I might add. Sometimes I wonder if these adventures ever happened, since it feels like a lifetime ago, but I have the photos and companions' comments to prove it.

Back in 1978, after three years in the Congo, my then husband and I flew to Europe and traveled for six months in many countries. Lots of stories there—but not for this book. The plan was to purchase a Land Rover in England and take that across the Sahara desert in order to eventually meet up with my dad and one of his camping buddies about seven months later in Kenya. That we accomplished but without the Land Rover. We traversed the Sahara from north to south via Algeria and what was then Niger (now Burkina Faso) by hitchhiking and catching rides with fellow travelers. For the first part of the crossing, after being creative about hitching rides, sometimes with truckers, we connected with a ragtag group of folks to make the next hop to Tamanrasset in southern Algeria. In the desert, for both safety and companionship reasons, two or three vehicles usually caravan and travel together. This particular group we joined included a French printer, his Cameroonian wife, a Swiss shepherd and his girlfriend, two French mechanics, a German gynecologist, and an Algerian medical student on vacation. Talk about a motley crew of personalities and skills. My husband volunteered to drive the spare Land Rover that the printer and his wife were taking back to her hometown in Cameroon.

I wrote a small book, now out of print, called *Saharan Kaleidoscope* about those adventures and the spiritual awakening sparked by the vastness of time and space in the open desert. Let's just say that it is no accident that many of the world's major religions have started in that openness where there is no pollution or technology to insulate you from the grandeur of the Universe.

Many parts of this journey feel surreal, like a year out of time. The only way to travel that kind of distance under arduous conditions is to travel light and be able to shed excess baggage as you go. I had a small backpack with three outfits and a little carrying case for our cooking equipment. I left all my travel clothes for Europe there and selected appropriate ones for the next stage of the journey.

I believe dreams can share with us powerful messages we may not be open to hearing on a more conscious level. During the cancer adventure, I had a series of five dreams that really resonated about the process I was undertaking. These dreams were usually set in airports, often leaving one country for another, and they always involved suitcases. In all of them, my baggage was lost or misplaced, or I had to make a conscious decision to abandon my possessions in order to progress or move on. Dreams can often present us with subtle insights and metaphors for what is going on in our lives. However, there was no subtlety in these five repeated versions. It was like, "Do you get it now?" "Now?" "Now?" "Now?" Remember the two-by-eight strategy? These dreams were a variation on that theme to ensure that I got the point about traveling light. During the course of this year, I have continued to let go of perceived limitations, old belief systems, any hurts and regrets, and emotionally draining conditions and people I was still carrying as baggage. I am convinced that this releasing was an integral part of my healing. I am not completely done, since this is an adventure of a lifetime, but I am a lot lighter. If you have ever backpacked, you know that the full tube of toothpaste that seemed like a good idea at the time becomes very heavy over the miles. The higher you climb and the longer the distance, the greater the burden. Remember to travel lightly and with companions that you can trust and count on, since you never know what is just around the corner.

Reflection, Playtime, and Continuing the Journey
What can you release on your journey to lighten the load? Is it clutter in your life, both literally and figuratively? Is it out-dated beliefs and coping strategies that served you well in the moment but no longer fit? Is it people and conversations that drain you? Remember all the European clothes I jettisoned before approaching the Sahara?

> *If you want to go fast, go alone. If you want to go far, travel together.*
>
> —*AFRICAN PROVERB*

Timing Is Everything

Due to sandstorms, there are only certain windows of time that you can safely cross the Sahara in the north-south direction. That timing may have shifted a bit now, but during 1978, the months of January and February were best. Miss that opening of opportunity and it could be hard, dangerous slogging, if you could make it at all. Much of our planning for that year focused on making that window. It influenced our ultimate decision not to buy the Land Rover and to move faster than we had originally intended. It also informed whom we chose to travel with, how we traveled, and how long we lingered in certain spots.

Reflection, Playtime, and Continuing the Journey
What risks do you need to assess, and what timing is mission critical for you on your adventure? Can you wait to see what evolves? Or do you have to move quickly and with focused purpose in your decision-making?

Adventure Highlights

- Rescuing two broken-down Land Rovers with stranded passengers and lending them mechanical assistance. The key was that the passengers had strung aluminum foil on sand ladders stacked on top of the vehicles, and we could see from a great distance the foil flashing in the sunlight. Talk about innovating on the ground!
- Circling the wagons at night (literally pulling the vehicles into a tight circle) around the campfire in order to protect the women in the party from visits by the Algerian soldiers at a nearby military outpost.
- Changing innumerable flat tires. The two French mechanics that were a part of our ragtag entourage at the time could change a flat tire in less than five minutes. Evenings were spent repairing the day's spare for the next day's journey.
- Sleeping on the roof of the Land Rover in sleeping bags some nights due to the presence of scorpions and other venomous creatures.
- Drinking gallons of water a day and never seeing it again except as sweat.

- Wearing sweaters and lots of clothing, even in 110- to 120-degree weather, both for cultural reasons and to trap the moisture evaporating from your body.
- Eating extraordinary homemade meals prepared over the campfire by the Cameroonian woman from the provisions in her truck. Meals appeared from nothing almost like magic.
- Enjoying the way the sand glistened like snow in the early-morning sunlight.
- Endless attention to jerry cans filled with water and gasoline. These are precious, life-sustaining resources in the open desert.
- Playful visits with touring Tuareg nomads and their baby camels as they caravanned past our vehicles.
- The full Milky Way as magic on display in a way I have never experienced before or since.

They say your most potent memories have strong emotions that go with them. My recollections of my two months in the deep Sahara are indelibly etched in my memory all these years later. It felt like a time of continuous peak experiences. And if I believed in past lives, I would say that one of mine was spent as a Tuareg nomad and that I had come home on that journey.

Reflection, Playtime, and Continuing the Journey
What are your favorite or most precious memories on your journey? Please capture them in a journal or blog. You never know when they may be useful to you or someone else!

Try a values-clarification exercise. While on the ranch in eastern Washington, we almost lost everything twice due to raging forest fires. I used to drive around with two boxes in the trunk that represented all that I would consider precious if I had to let go of most of my possessions. What would go in your two boxes? What relationships would you keep that are renewing and sustaining?

On Track or Off Track?

THE DIFFERENCE BETWEEN LIFE AND DEATH

One of the many lessons from crossing the Sahara was the need to constantly recalibrate and find your way forward. While there is now a paved road for most of the territory we crossed in 1978, back then, once you got past Tamanrasset in southern Algeria, roads did not exist. There were vehicle tracks going in all directions and abandoned, burned-out cars as a warning to travelers. It was not clear what had happened to the occupants. Did they perish, or did fellow voyagers rescue them? Sometimes the way forward was unclear, and we needed to stop, stand on top of the car, and search the skyline to see where a particular track went. Was it a detour, a dead end, or a well-traveled route? Was it a real oasis on the horizon, promising a respite, or a mirage fooling a very thirsty traveler?

Just in case there is a breakdown, seasoned desert travelers always caravan with another vehicle. That is a smart move. Remember what I said about traveling with an elite team? I wish I could say that we followed that guidance all the time. But we did not on the second half of the Sahara crossing, and it added to the risk when we got stuck. We needed to get across the border since our visas were due to expire, and we could not wait around for our previous travel companions. We needed to keep moving to get to Agadez. So I "worked the crowd" of other fellow travelers at an outpost in Tamanrasset and found two Germans, originally from Czechoslovakia, who were driving a telephone truck across the desert with the intention of selling it on the other side. We teamed up with them in one vehicle, which was expedient but not too bright. Sometimes you do what you gotta do, assess the risks, and keep on trekking.

Once, as a solo vehicle, we were bogged down in deep sand, shoveling, shoveling, and shoveling for what seemed like hours in the desert heat. Then out of nowhere, an elegant Tuareg nomad woman appeared with a jerry can of water and her young son. She greeted us warmly, and in a mixture of broken French and sign language, she asked if we had any paper and pens, since she wanted to teach her son to write. Miraculously, we did, as another traveler had given us a hot tip that Bic pens made great gifts and were a much-appreciated trading commodity. What a reframe from being bogged down and struggling to appreciating the beauty of the human spirit in the most improbable of circumstances. Needless to say, we soon freed ourselves and were on our way.

Many times, we relied on gut, intuition, and just plain luck. "May the force be with you"—and it was. That force got us through sandstorms that kept us trapped in a camper for three days. It got me through a bout of dysentery when only bottled Coca Cola kept me alive for several days, through almost being kidnapped by Palestinian terrorists, and through almost being sold for camels at a watering hole. And it got us through interactions with Algerian border guards who claimed our visas for Niger were fake (they were not) in an attempt to extract a ransom or "pound of flesh." To state the obvious, once you have really committed to the journey, there is no going back. You learn to innovate on the ground, marshal resources you did not even know you had, and just keep moving.

For me, that year of travails and travel gave me the confidence that I could handle almost anything. It was trial by fire in many ways, with moments of joy I have not fully described here. Adventures and journeys are an empowering metaphor for me when I encounter a growth opportunity like cancer. Context is everything, and if I frame it as an adventure, a different part of me—not the scared lady who wants to play it safe—kicks in, and off we go. At that point, I am finally able to let the excitement and risks of not knowing the outcome or all the turns and twists on the road propel me forward.

Reflection, Playtime, and Continuing the Journey
On your cancer journey, where are you on track or off track? Get real about this, since it can make a big difference. If there is no roadmap, how will you find your way forward across your own desert?

Make a list of challenges you have already encountered in your life. A divorce? A bad car accident? A very sick child? Caring for an elderly parent? The death of someone close to you? Being let go from a job you love? Adventures come in all flavors, both chosen and not chosen.

Now make a list of how you overcame those challenges. What friends, inner guidance, and outside resources helped you on the journey? These resources can help you now as well. We all have them. It is often just a matter of recognizing them, putting them in place, and choosing to use them.

Rafting the Grand Canyon
at Flood Level

Back in early 1983, during the time when I was living in Washington, DC, I had the opportunity to journey the Grand Canyon for twelve days on small rafts with a commercial rafting company. Each boat holds four passengers and a guide who rows with long oars. A good friend of mine at the time had done a lot of rafting and had connections, so I went along as staff, essentially as a spare cook and bottle washer, while he rowed the baggage boat. That meant, among other tasks, getting up at the crack of dawn to have a sumptuous breakfast ready for the guests. The trip started at Lees Ferry and ended before Lake Mead, and it was the experience of a lifetime in many unanticipated ways.

At the bottom of the canyon, where stone walls five thousand feet high encase the Colorado River, everything is magnified—the colors, the sounds, and especially the intensity of the emotions. It is hard to actually put words to the feelings, since they are very primal, but it often felt as if my emotions and everyone else's literally reverberated off the walls of the canyon. Being aware of this (I had been prewarned by my friend), noticing the impact, and not taking it personally were key. Sounds a little bit like the cancer adventure, doesn't it?

Once you are on the water, there is only one place to disembark before the final takeout. It is about halfway down the route and a very tough hike back to the top. Either you get off in the middle of the ride with unknown consequences when you are on a group trip, or you ride the flow to the final destination. Remember not getting off the roller coaster in the middle of the ride? It is the same analogy.

When we first got on the river, the water level was at its highest point in decades. In fact, water was being let out of spillways of the Glen Canyon dam to prevent the dam from breaking. Even the seasoned professional boatmen and women had never experienced the water this high, so it became an unknown river they had never run.

A hole occurs where the water reverses on itself and forms a treacherous place that can drown swimmers and suck down or flip rafts. Holes can take many forms, and all are dangerous and must be avoided or navigated very, very carefully. At these water levels, the holes were either humongous or totally washed out, and often it was impossible to tell which they were until you were right on top of them. Our guides did the best scouting they could, but sometimes they needed to just trust their instincts and the small indicators of which way to go, even when we could not see the way ahead. I remember one time when the force of the water was rushing so hard at me that I could not see my friend just a couple of feet ahead of me in the boat! All I could do was hang on for dear life and try to stay in the raft, hoping we would soon be on the other side of these particular rapids before entering another one.

There were people dying on the river at the time. There were whirlpools sucking logs down into the vortex and spitting them to the surface a quarter of a mile later. At least one big motorized pontoon boat plowed through the Crystal Rapids, hit a big hole, overturned, and dumped all its passengers into the raging river. Good thing we were a couple hundred yards downstream and were able to pick them up. Our boatmen rescued everyone. That particular boat floated about one and a half miles before coming to rest on a sandbar.

Stay light and agile, and don't be arrogant and try to power through obstacles thinking that past practices allow you to have it all handled. Cancer can be a tricky disease, the treatments uncertain and evolving to fit the situation. Staying nimble and in tune with your body can impact the outcome. There was more than one time when I needed to reach out to the doctors on call on a weekend or late at night to get their advice on a potential emergency. I called, and they were patient and knowledgeable. We avoided a major crisis. Staying present and attuned and "reading the river" made all the difference in a smooth ride versus a traumatic overturn and setback.

Treat each day as if it may be your last. If it's not cancer, it might be that pickup truck that runs a red light and totals your car. That has happened to me twice. It's great advice, and it means you really savor that morning cup of coffee!

When we hit that midway point where some of us could have hiked out, we were faced with a big decision. We chose not to leave and then were committed to the rest of the journey. None of us, even the most experienced boatmen, knew what lay ahead of us. The river was rising, and the territory was an unknown version of previously well-traveled and marked milestones. And we as staff needed to remain and project calm so that our passengers did not freak out. Total freak-out would only make it harder on everyone. They trusted us to get them off the river safely and alive, and we had to trust ourselves too. We almost missed our Diamond Creek takeout point due to the high water, which would have meant a few more days of river running to get to Lake Mead. But with valiant effort and an all-out push, we finally made it to shore. Talk about time to celebrate!

There is nothing like risk and jumping into the river of the unknown to clarify your priorities and encourage embracing and appreciating the small pleasures of life. Good coffee and fireside conversation; a refreshing, cool dunk in the river in one hundred-degree temperatures; a warm sleeping bag, and the fact that the rattlesnake did not curl up in it with you...sound familiar?

Reflection, Playtime, and Continuing the Journey

What will allow you to stay in the boat, even with everything that is rushing at you?

While this story is about twelve days on the Colorado River, ask yourself what you would do if you knew you only had twelve days left. This has actually happened to two friends of mine. They got a diagnosis, and three weeks later, they were gone. What would you do with your twelve days? How would you use them? Whom would you contact with acknowledgments, and whom would you tell that you love them? What promises would you fulfill? What regrets would clear? You get the idea. It is an opportunity to totally clear and clean up your life so that you have a totally fresh start on your next adventure.

A Dead End or a Profound Opening?

This chapter is a story unto itself as well as a bridge to part 3 and the unfolding of the next phase of both the book and my life. In 2014, after government budget cuts forced me to leave a job I loved, I was headed to Mongolia. If you have already been a Peace Corps volunteer in good standing or are in a critical medical field, you can apply for a short-term, one-year assignment. I was ready to shift my somewhat comfortable, predicable life, shake off the dust, get my blood flowing, and create some new experiences.

My dear father had transitioned, and my original goal in moving to Virginia Beach was complete. I figured that if I was going to do one last overseas assignment and adventure, the time was now. Be careful what you ask for!

I had completed the application process, passed the preliminary medical screening, received my Mongolian assignment, and knew the neighborhood where I was to have a tiny studio in the capital, Ulaanbaatar. I was moving forward into what I considered a dream job of coaching colleagues in a not-for-profit to promote entrepreneurship and Mongolian start-ups. I was psyched and ready to go! I was sorting through my personal effects and furniture, downsizing yet again, and had my primo storage unit all picked out. I was reading the English version of the Mongolian news online every day and had already networked my way into some very interesting circles via a consultant friend from Seattle who had done some work there. My yurt fantasy from college was finally going to be fulfilled, and I was boning up on Mongolian history. I felt as if I was practically on the plane and poised for takeoff.

And then bam! Another two-by-eight! A dead end in a maze! My assignment, along with those for two other more senior folks, was abruptly cancelled. Even the Peace Corps recruiter at headquarters was stunned. Apparently, three key staff in country had left unexpectedly, and the group of new volunteers already in place needed to be trained on a tight timeline. The organizers felt they could not support the three of us in the nonstandard assignments. Good call from an operational and management perspective, and conceptually, I totally understood and appreciated it. However, personally, I was dazed, and it felt like a real blow. The future I had been creating and was stepping into dissolved with a phone call from the DC-based recruiter. I had already finished my current job and was now in a void that felt like an abyss.

I started walking one of our local beaches one day very soon after the call. As I walked, I kept hearing a whisper of "HeartMath." Now, I had loosely and one might even say sporadically been practicing the heart-based coherence tools for a few years. I was familiar with and totally appreciative of the work and research the organization had done over the past two decades. But I had not been consistent in my practice and had not reaped all the possible benefits.

Several times in my life, I have had a door open almost magically in an unexpected fashion. What unfolded was another case of synchronicity, and I have learned to lean into and trust that process. Years before, I had dreamed of being a HeartMath coach and trainer, but at that time, they were not certifying independent consultants like me. Immediately after getting off the beach, I went to the website and discovered that after almost seventeen years, they had recently opened up the certification. I called right away and had an amazing conversation with Jeff at the not-for-profit wing, and the rest is history—dream fulfilled. It was like having twenty green lights show up in a row and being in the flow. When that happens, I trust my intuition and know that I am on the right path.

I did both my coach and trainer certifications over the next several months and now use the HeartMath system as the foundation for all my executive coaching of high-leverage, high-impact individuals committed to making a difference in the world.

And by the way, my former project manager found some spare contract money and was able to hire me back for a few months on a different contract so that my financial needs were taken care of while I completed my training in the evenings. Sweet! Yet another example of how the Universe works if we only get out of the way!

Using HeartMath skills was and is a core piece of my cancer healing and ongoing resilience. No accident there. I didn't expect to be my own case study on the value of resilience, but now I have "street cred" with my clients. One of my beliefs is that we all have the resources we need to thrive no matter what the circumstances. Sometimes we have to dig deep or be willing to learn, but we are equipped for whatever two-by-eights come our way. I also focus on the energy of what I chose to create and try not to be attached to the form in which it shows up. I am in fact still in my dream job—it just looks different from what I had envisioned in Mongolia.

How did not going to Mongolia save my life? The aggressive tumors had not yet appeared at the time I was to leave for my assignment. They were not detected until I had a three-dimensional mammogram several months later. That level of screening would not have happened in Mongolia, and who knows what the outcome would have been. Maybe I would still be here or maybe not. In any case, it is on to the next adventure!

Part Three:
The Adventure Continues

Back in part 1, in the chapter called "The Trigger," I shared a critical event in my life and how I was given a choice to "go big or go home." That choice still resonates with me on a daily basis. What that actually looks like in the particulars of my future is still germinating, and in my new "allowing" perspective, that is perfect and is my growth edge. If you are looking for a detailed outline of what is next, I cannot give it to you.

Framing cancer and life as an adventure story takes some of the trauma and drama out of the picture or at least puts it into perspective. When you claim you are on an adventure, you expect the ups and downs, the mishaps, and sudden twists in the road. They all become part of the stories you can tell your grandchildren, and with enough perspective, you can see those hurdles yield the richness of challenges overcome and lessons learned. No bumps, no stories.

Back in 1986, I sold my townhouse in Washington, DC, put everything in storage, and moved to London to work for a British consulting firm for a few months. When I came back to DC, I intuitively knew I had a three-week window of time in which to make a powerful decision about my future. Was I going to settle back down into a fairly predictable life as a DC management consultant, or would I use this interlude as a catapult into an unknown and uncertain future? I chose the latter. Everyone said, "You can't do that. It is too risky."

I replied, "Just watch me!" I surrounded myself with friends who encouraged me, and I gave the naysayers little of my time and attention. See any parallels with your cancer adventure? I flew to Seattle with no job and no real place to live, and I created a whole new life in the Pacific Northwest for the next twenty years. I started a small consulting firm of my own and had great clients. I got to run a llama ranch, and I got married on a six-day llama trek in the Cascades. None of that would have been possible if I had stuck to the trajectory of my life in DC. I won't say it was always easy, but it was rewarding, fulfilling, and came with its own set of adventures.

Who knows what two-by-eights might show up and how I will dance with them? If they do, I will frame them as an adventure, since I know that is what works for me personally. What I do know is that we live in an uncertain time. Back in the 1990s, the US Army War College coined the acronym VUCA—volatility, uncertainty, complexity, and ambiguity—as the basis for understanding military strategy. Now that phrase has made its way into the business world, and you can find articles in the *Harvard Business Review* giving guidance on how to stay agile and productive in the current VUCA economy and business climate. Since this book is about resilience, courage, and transformation, however, I prefer to define VUCA as vision, understanding, clarity, and agility. Words matter, and those are the ones I choose to use.

Perhaps I was root bound and required repotting for new growth. Certainly, I am now in a very expansive container! About halfway through the yearlong journey,

I heard whispers of "In a year, your life will be unrecognizable." At this writing, I still do not know exactly what that means, since there are still several months to go. I am living in curiosity and expectancy and am exercising my trust muscle that "all is well."

This adventure has called me to reassess my definition of success as well as what that looks and feels like at this phase of my life postcancer. Elements of our current culture define success as wealth and status, and our sense of worthiness is often shaped by how we feel we measure up on those scales. It is about accomplishments and material accumulation. That is changing for many, and what I am choosing for myself now is deep connection and spirituality. I am using my why as a GPS as I navigate my choices, and I am continuously creating my life and future on a daily basis. Peter Drucker, the management guru, says, "The best way to predict the future is to create it." Very wise words. I can appreciate the irony that while I have never considered myself a writer or aspired to be one, I am being led to stay present in my life and to literally and figuratively write a whole new story.

Freedom has been choosing me. At the church I attend, we have an end-of-the-year ritual called a burning-bowl ceremony. You write on small pieces of paper all those things you would like to release from the past year, add the papers to the bowl, ignite them, and watch them dissolve into ashes. But nature abhors a vacuum; it is important to replace what you release with what you are intending and choosing for the new year. So after burning the papers, you receive a small, hand-cut white stone quarried near Bethlehem. After a period of deep mediation, you write one word on the stone that represents your intention for the energy of the newness you are embracing. Even in the midst of the cancer adventure and long before this book was conceived, my word was freedom.

What is my new freedom? For me freedom is an attitude, and it is about who I am being rather than what I am doing. It is about continuously choosing, moment by moment. Remember the Viktor Frankl quote at the beginning of the book? That is where we source our power.

I choose as my passport to freedom:

Embracing joy
Cultivating aliveness
Allowing the unfolding
Challenging limits
Encouraging boldness
Facilitating deep connection
Thriving

What do you choose? Do you frame your two-by-eight as a little bump in the road, as a disaster, or as a catapult into a new life? Which choice moves you into inspired action?

And promise me you will go and buy yourself a kaleidoscope. It is one of the most powerful tools of transformation on the planet. Then play with it. Give it a shake, a big twist, and a gentle nudge. Notice all the shifting patterns—some magnificent, all intriguing. That is what is possible both for you and for me. We are not stuck. All it takes is a nudge—or sometimes a two-by-eight—to launch us into what is truly possible!

Bon voyage.

Reflection, Playtime, and Continuing the Journey

How can you use your resources and skills from past adventures on this one?

What if you frame your cancer and treatments as a time-out to slow down and assess your life and decide what is really important? Focus not just on the bucket list but on relationships and your why as well.

What is your *next adventure? Get an adventure journal, or create a vision board. Go to Barnes and Noble and thumb through magazines, or have fun on Pinterest. It does not have to be exotic travel. It could be that novel or short story you have always thought about. It could be starting your own business. Just be open to what wonderful things might be emerging in your life because of your adventure with cancer.*

Acknowledgments

When on an adventure, it is important to feel you are part of a community and a tribe. I am blessed to be a member of several tribes, and they all supported me in wonderful and unique ways.

I want to acknowledge all of you for being companions on this adventure and encouraging, supporting, and listening to me when I needed it most. The hugs were great and very much needed. Thank you. I could not have made the journey without you. And to anyone I accidentally missed, a big thank-you as well.

First of all, I thank my family tribe, comprising my sister, Tina Batty; her husband, Gene; and their sons, Travis Batty and Brandon Batty, plus the dogs and all the extended family and children. Tina and Gene, thank you for all those nights after surgeries and chemotherapy that you fed me and let me sleep in the spare bedroom, plus all the times you drove me to treatments when I could not do it myself. Words cannot fully express my gratitude and appreciation.

A shout-out to Valerie Jones, who did amazing handholding and gave me phenomenal support and guidance on the steps to bring this book into existence.

Thanks to my tribe of friends both near and far: Diane King; Jeni Miller; Suzan Thompson; Susan Henson; AnnaMarie Smith-Butz; the ladies of the Lake (Gale, Susan, Sandy, and Lydia); Angelika Greenhalgh;

Barbara Lewis; Michele Ewing; Karen Eagle; Cecilia Finnigan; Terry Pottinger; Valerie Jones, Christopher Naughton, and their team at the American Law Journal; Scott Chierepko; Alex Then; Elari Onawa; Sandy True; Barb Giger; Ryan Rico; Sandy True and Kathy Damm.

I am grateful to my tribe at the transition institute for Special Operations Forces: Jeff Pottinger, Joe Musselman, Mike Turkenkopf, Kristen Robillard, Kerianne McGovern, all the staff and amazing coaches, and especially group seven (you know who you are). Thank you for allowing me to be a part of the tribe when I needed it most!

To my HeartMath tribe who supported me in this year transformation: Jeff Goelitz, Tricia Hoffman, Brian Kabaker, Rollin McCraty, Katherine Floriano, Barb Hudak, Michele Lash, Kimberly Gray, Ryan Dana, and several others. Your belief in me and my healing was priceless.

I thank my tribe at Unity Renaissance, especially Rev. Paula Mekdeci.

And to my truly amazing healing tribe composed of my oncologist and surgeon: your loving and expert care made this possible and helped me navigate a complex system of care. And a big heartfelt *wow* to my team of integrative therapists and healers: Mari Kelley, Anana Integre, Bryan Gilpin, Joyce Hawkes, Dr. Jeanine Lex, Alex Then, Dr. Cathy Good, and Jeni Miller. Our work together created miracles!

My tribe of HeartMath and executive coaching clients gave me love, patience, and support during the whole process. Thank you for being my cheerleaders!

Denise Rang, my hairstylist, totally understands what it means to shear a Leo's mane, and she gave me encouragement as my wild, now-gray hair grew back.

Thanks to my Friday night tribe at the Town Center City Club.

I am grateful for Melanie Williams, my first Peace Corps post-mate in the Congo and lifelong friend. We recently reunited in person after more than forty years. I could not have made it through that first year without you!

Special thanks to Paul Dorvel for being a great companion and husband on many of these adventures in Africa, especially crossing the Sahara.

Made in the USA
Middletown, DE
11 November 2017